PROGRAMMING MODELS for PARALLEL SYSTEMS

 **WILEY** SERIES IN PARALLEL COMPUTING
Publishers Since 1807

SERIES EDITORS:

R.G. Babb, Oregon Graduate Center, USA

J.W. de Bakker, *Centrum voor Wiskunde en Informatica, The Netherlands*

M. Hennessy, *University of Sussex, UK*

D. Simpson, *Brighton Polytechnic, UK*

PROGRAMMING MODELS for PARALLEL SYSTEMS

Shirley A. Williams
University of Reading, UK

WILEY

JOHN WILEY & SONS

Chichester · New York · Brisbane · Toronto · Singapore

Other Wiley Editorial Offices

John Wiley & Sons, Inc., 605 Third Avenue,
New York, NY 10158-0012, USA

Jacaranda Wiley Ltd, G.P.O. Box 859, Brisbane,
Queensland 4001, Australia

John Wiley & Sons (Canada) Ltd, 22 Worcester Road,
Rexdale, Ontario M9W 1L1, Canada

John Wiley & Sons (SEA) Pte Ltd, 37 Jalan Pemimpin 05-04,
Block B, Union Industrial Building, Singapore 2057

Library of Congress Cataloging-in-Publication Data:

Williams, Shirley A.
    Programming models for parallel systems/Shirley A. Williams.
        p.   cm.—(Wiley series in parallel computing)
    Includes bibliographical references.
    ISBN 0 471 92304 4
    1. Parallel programming (Computer science)   I. Title.
    II. Series.
    QA76.642.W55   1990   89-70543
    004'.35—dc20   CIP

British Library Cataloguing in Publication Data:

Williams, Shirley A.
    Programming models for parallel systems.–(Wiley series
    in parallel computing).
    1. Computer systems. Parallel-processor systems.
    Programming
    I. Title
    005.1

    ISBN 0 471 92304 4

Phototypeset by Dobbie Typesetting Limited, Plymouth, Devon
Printed in Great Britain by Courier International, Tiptree, Essex

To my family

Contents

Preface

This book is based on my personal views of parallel processing developed over the past 15 years initially at Loughborough University of Technology and then at Reading University. The material brought together here is based on research work and taught courses given over that time.

Not all workers in the field of parallel processing will agree with all the contents of this book. Twice within the last month I have been told that parallel processing would not be used if sequential computers were fast enough; I do not share this view. While it is true people may not invest in expensive parallel processors, some will still use parallelism to represent their problem in what they consider a natural form. There is a great deal of work currently under way in the area of parallel processing, funded by industry as well as by national and international initiatives, and the reader must expect that there will be changes of views within the next few years. Indeed a difficulty I have discovered in agreeing to write a book is that during the period of time from the original idea to completion my views have changed. This makes producing a coherent piece of work difficult—but, I hope for the reader's sake, not impossible.

After studying the material the reader (whether undergraduate, postgraduate, research worker or industrialist) should be able to formulate answers to the following questions:

1. Why use parallelism?
2. Why are there so many models of parallelism?
3. Why attempt to alter the model?

My answers to these questions are presented in the final chapter of this book.

Shirley A. Williams
September, 1989

Acknowledgements

I would like to thank all my past and present colleagues and students at Reading for their help with my work, by discussion and criticism. Thanks must go especially to Jennifer Stapleton and an unknown reviewer for their many helpful reviews and comments on earlier versions of this work, and to Sylvia Tompkins for many helpful discussions and much encouragement.

Finally I would like to thank my family and friends for their encouragement and support; especially my husband Roy and our children: Thomas, Joseph and Susannah.

1 *Introduction*

Studying the history of computers is a fascinating exercise. Computers can be considered either to have a very short history (essentially starting from the Second World War). Alternatively their history can be traced back to when first a man scratched marks on the ground to aid his memory [Evans 1981].

Similarly the history of parallel computers can be considered to have a very brief history (the first papers on the concept of parallel processing were published in the late 1950s [Gill 1958]). Alternatively their history can be traced back to when first a man used marks on the ground to aid his memory while a woman picked up small stones to aid her memory.

One of the major landmarks on the path to computerization was the American 1880 census. An army of clerks were employed to analyse the results. They were still calculating seven years later, by which time the population had changed enormously and the figures were no longer valid. The Census Bureau held a competition to find a better way of recording and counting the population. As a result of the competition, Hollerith's Tabulating Machine was used to help calculate the results of the 1890 census. Whatever the difficulties with the enormity of taking a census in the 1880s, strategies must have existed to divide the task of analysing the results between many people, who could then work independently, but together (in parallel) on the one problem.

Many sets of tables were produced by such armies of clerks; Victorian novels frequently refer to several clerks together in small offices working on accounts. Old dictionaries refer to such clerks as *computers*. So in the last century there were many examples of *computers* working in parallel.

Unfortunately the advent and following popularity of the electronic computer forced a need to think *sequentially* if problems were to be solved. This was due to the principle now called the Von Neumann concept: that is, the computer executes one statement and then control passes to the next statement. So the algorithms that represented the solution to a problem were forced to fit a mould dictated by the computer that was to solve the problem. Unless this mould can be broken non-sequential computers can never be fully utilized. Remember, four or five generations ago, parallel processing was quite acceptable, so surely it shouldn't be too difficult to break out of the sequential mould.

1.1 A PARALLEL PROBLEM

Before going any further consider the following problem:
Given a sequence of values α_i:

$$\alpha_1 \alpha_2 \ldots \alpha_n$$

Find the maximum value of the sums of the subsequences, i.e. the maximum value of S, where:

$$S = \sum_{i=j}^{k} \alpha_i, \quad 1 \le j \le k \le n$$

e.g. for the sequence: 1 2 1 3 4 the maximum subsequence value is 11.
and for: 2 −4 5 6 −1 the maximum value is also 11.
Can you write an algorithm that will produce the required results?
Is your algorithm inherently sequential?
   A full discussion of how such algorithms should be specified (as opposed to implemented is given in Ibrahim et al [1989]. This is a very interesting topic but somewhat beyond the scope of the present text.

1.2 PEOPLE AS PROCESSORS

Consider that there are a number of people available to help with calculating the maximum value of the sums of subsequences.[1] Will your algorithm help you to utilize these people? At this point there are a number of questions that should be asked:

- How many people?
- Where are they?
- How bright are they?
- How are they going to know what to do?
- How are they going to let us know they have finished and any results they have achieved?

Consider the case where there is a large class of students (almost an infinite supply of people). Then the sequence could be displayed on a board at the front of the room and different students could be asked to calculate each of the possible subsequences. When a student finishes she puts her hand in the air. When all students calculating have finished, one at random is asked

---

[1]This is a *fun* exercise to start off a course in parallel processing.

for his sum. Then the class is asked if anyone has a greater sum; if no one does then that sum is the answer, otherwise you consider only the group with larger sums and choose one at random and cycle round until the maximum subsequence is isolated.

A number of minor variations can be used with the above example. Once two students have calculated their sums you can compare for the greater, even though other students are still calculating (care is needed not to distract those performing mental arithmetic). If there are less students than sums to be performed, once a student finishes she can be given another sum to perform, while there are calculations to be done (clever scheduling helps here: allocation of the longest sums first will reduce the chance of a bottleneck created by the most difficult sum being given as the last calculation and everyone else waiting for that student to finish).

This is only one possible approach. What if there wasn't a board and students could only communicate by passing notes to the person they are sat next to? Then given the same number of students as there are elements in the list, the students could be sat in a row and given the value of the element in the sequence which corresponds to their position in the row.

The algorithm they follow could be that each student passes their value to the student on their right. Each then adds his own value to the one received to get a *sum*; this *sum* is compared to the student's own value and the larger passed to the right. This is repeated $n-1$ more times. Now one of the students will definitely know the value of the maximum subsequence, and so the first student in the row can be instructed to pass what he thinks is the maximum value to the right, the remainder of the row when they receive a value compare it to what they have and pass the larger along. The value passed on by the last student in the row is the maximum subsequence.

A class of six-year-olds would require much more direction. Their teacher would previously have prepared pieces of paper, one for each possible combination of numbers and on each sheet she would have clearly written the corresponding values. Each child is given a piece of paper with their numbers on; those with only one number leave the room; the remainder are then instructed to add the first two numbers together. All children with only two numbers would then be sent out of the room and the remainder would add in their third number, and so on. When the addition was completed all the children would be called back and polled for the highest sum. If the teacher doubted the class's mathematical capabilities, then the same sequence could be given to several children and the answer that was achieved by the most of them would be taken to be correct!

A group of professors may just be given the problem specification and left to determine the method of solution and the answer without further direction.

All these groups are homogeneous (excepting the infants' teacher) the problems associated with heterogeneous groups is, in general, beyond the scope of this book. A question the reader should now ask is:

Is any one of the solutions above the **best**?

The last solution (i.e. the professors) is probably the easiest to represent but is of no use if the resources available are a class of six-year-olds. For a given group of people it is possible to ask if this is a realistic task to set these people or if this is the best algorithm to use given this group.

1.3   MACHINES AS PROCESSORS

Parallel processing machines are constructed from a number of processors; like the groups of people described they conform to a variety of models. There are a number of classifications of these models, each of which can be composed of a number of processing elements. Here five distinct hardware models are identified:

- Sequential
- Processor array
- Pipeline processors
- Shared memory
- Message passing

These models are also represented in software.

There are proposals for many other models of parallelism; however, the above five categories can always be mapped into from any other models. Thus these five are the basic models. The two other most popular models are:

- Object-oriented
- Functional

Other models have also been proposed, some encompassing various aspects of the above others to meet specific application needs. Briefly:

- The sequential model is the conventional model
- The processor array reflects lots of *stupid* processors obeying a controller
- The pipeline is a line of specialist processors that information is passed down
- A shared memory model represents many processors working on a common pool of data
- A message-passing processor represents many processors working together but communicating according to a well-defined protocol
- Object-oriented models consider the data more important than the processes
- A functional model describes the relationship between the input data and the output data

The above are merely thumbnail sketches and should be read with a pinch of salt!

An alternative description (also amenable to the application of salt) is now presented.

1.4 A COMPARISON OF PROGRAMMING MODELS FOR PARALLEL PROCESSING (or a Kitchen Sink Drama)

Consider the scenario:

The family has just finished their traditional English Sunday lunch; all that remains is to clear the table, wash up and put the clean things away. There are a number of different solutions to this problem, depending on the number of helpers (processors) available. There are also a number of ways in which a solution can be described.

1.4.1 A Sequential Model Using One Processor

- Dad takes the children to the park
- While Mum clears the table, washes the pots, dries them and puts them away

1.4.2 A Sequential Model Using Four Processors

- Dad clears the table, when he has finished
- Joe[1] washes up, when he has finished
- Tom dries the pots, when he has finished
- Susie puts them away

  (Mum is busy writing her book!)

1.4.3 A Pipeline Using Four Processors

- Dad gets an item, gives it to Joe and goes to get the next item
- Joe washes it, gives it to Tom and waits to accept the next item from Dad
- Tom dries it, gives it to Susie and waits to accept the next item from Joe
- Susie puts it away and waits for the next item from Tom

---

[1]Note the difference between the **processor** called Joe and the **process** of washing up. The **processor** Joe can undertake a number of different activities, given the right set of instructions (i.e. the description of the **process**). Certain processes may require specific processors, for instance only one processor may be able to handle the sharp knife, so a process of carving the joint must be allocated to the processor Dad.

This model allows parallelism as everyone can be working on different items at the same time. The system needs a lot of synchronization. If Joe takes five minutes to wash a burnt pan everyone else will be standing around waiting:

- Dad will be waiting to give the next item to Joe
- Tom will be waiting to receive the pan so that he can dry it
- Susie having put away the previous item Tom gave her, will be waiting to put the pan away

1.4.4   A Message-passing System

The description of the pipeline would also serve as a description of a message-passing system, the pots being the messages. A message-passing system will allow communication between any processes, not just communication in the one direction to one processor of a pipeline.

A message-passing system would be required to handle the following additional requirements:

- If an item is clean Dad gives it directly to Susie
- If Tom receives a dirty item he gives it back to Joe

1.4.5   The Use of Buffers

With the above two systems delays will be experienced because both processors must be willing to participate in a communication (e.g. Tom must be willing to accept a wet dish and Joe to give him one). This problem can be avoided by the use of a buffer (or draining board) in which messages (dishes) can be stacked. This doesn't totally alleviate the problem because at times the buffer will be empty and at other times the buffer will be full (a draining board is of a finite size).

1.4.6   Shared Memory

With the buffers described above it was assumed that it was private to the two parties communicating. There is a more general case where there is a shared memory. This could be seen as a large draining board on which dirty, wet and clean dishes could all be stacked. Care will obviously have to be exercised to ensure that there is no attempt to dry dirty dishes! At the other extreme there is private space that belongs to just one person and no one else can access without specific permission; for instance, pots actually in the washing-up bowl may be seen as in the private domain of the washer-up. This can be combined with the shared-space concept, that some dishes are accessible by only one person but others can be accessed by many.

4.7 A Processor Array

Assume that the family has a large number of helpers that are brainless clones, each with their own washing up bowl, tea towel, etc. Then each of these could help to quickly complete the chore, but because of their stupidity they will have to be closely supervised. A *boss* will direct their every move, and to make life simple they will all perform the same action at a time. Thus the *boss* will say 'fetch a dish' and they will all rush to the table and fetch a dish. She will then say 'wash it' and they will all wash their dish. And so on. If at any point the *boss* decides that she does not require all of the helpers to work she can direct them to ignore the next set of instructions. This will be useful if there are (say) only five glasses, which require washing in a particular manner, then the excess helpers remain idle rather than trying to wash the burnt pans in the same manner as the glasses!

4.8 An Object-oriented Approach

Instead of thinking about processors (people) it is possible to consider the objects (e.g. pots, cutlery, etc.). Consider one class of objects in detail: plates. There are many states a plate may be in (e.g. dirty on the table, clean in the cupboard). The outside world will be interested in what state a plate is in, it (she) will not be concerned about the operations that transform the plate's state. The operations on the object are defined internally to the object. Thus the operation of drying a plate may be to wipe it with a tea towel, stack it on the draining board or hold it in front of the fire. The operations will have to be carried out by processors (Dad and co.) but the issue of scheduling is independent of this approach.

Each class of objects will have its own operations defined, for instance the drying of a plate may be defined as stacking it on the draining board while the drying of a piece of cutlery may be done by a tea towel.

4.9 A Functional Model

A single function can be defined that will model the whole of the washing-up operation. The function is applied to the dirty dishes on the table (the input stream) and the result is the clean dishes in the cupboard. This can be decomposed into a number of smaller functions, many of which will be similar to the message-passing model described earlier.

The role of the washer-up (Joe) can be seen as a function that takes a stream of dirty dishes, applies the operations of the function and produces a stream of damp, clean dishes.

Functional models are often based on lazy evaluation (only those values that are needed are evaluated). So when Susie requires a dish to put away, she must demand it from Tom, who will in his turn demand a dish to dry from Joe, who will demand from Dad a dish to wash, so Dad must fetch a dish from the table.

There are a number of ways the single function of washing up can be decomposed. The above scheme with lazy evaluation does not obviously lead to any parallelism. A model with more potential parallelism would be if instead of Joe and Tom the family used an automatic dishwasher: as with Joe and Tom the machine would take an input of dirty dishes and produce an output of clean, dry dishes. The implementation of the dishwasher will simultaneously wash then dry all dishes, cutlery, pots and pans, but this is an *implementation detail*, which a *true* functional programmer would consider unimportant.

1.5 FLYNN'S CLASSIFICATIONS

There are a number of alternative ways in which parallel computers can be classified. The most quoted is that of Flynn [1966]; although this is now very dated it is worth quickly outlining the four areas so that the reader will understand terms such as MIMD that members of the parallel processing community are fond of bandying around.

Computer systems are said to fall into one of four classes:

1. *Single instruction stream–single data stream* (SISD)

2. *Single instruction stream–multiple data stream* (SIMD)

3. *Multiple instruction stream–single data stream* (MISD)

4. *Multiple instruction stream–multiple data stream* (MIMD)

The SISD computer is the conventional serial computer that executes one instruction at a time (Figure 1.1).

Figure 1.1 *Model of an SISD computer*

The SIMD computer category is used to describe processor arrays; it is also used sometimes to describe pipeline processors. Unfortunately the SISD and MISD models are sometimes also used to describe identical pipelines[1] (Figures 1.2 and 1.3).

The MIMD model is used to describe loosely coupled processors working on a single problem; however, it does not allow for the interconnection topology or the mechanism of sharing and protecting information (Figure 1.4).

The classifications SIMD and MIMD are useful generic terms to differentiate between processors that must all perform the same operation and those that can *do their own thing*.

---

[1]A gross generalization is to say that European pipelines are SIMD, while American ones are MISD!

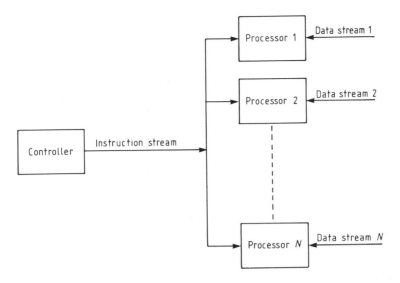

Figure 1.2   *Model of an SIMD computer*

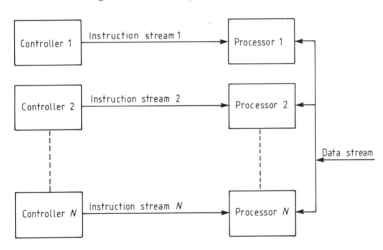

Figure 1.3   *Model of an MISD computer*

.6   CHAPTER REVIEW

- Parallel processing is doing more than one thing at a time
- Processors have differing capabilities
- There are five distinct models:
  —Sequential
  —Processor array

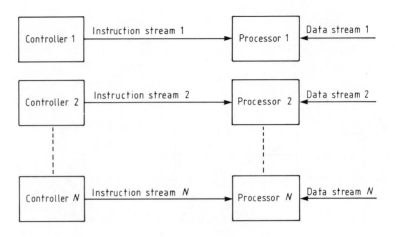

Figure 1.4   Model of an MIMD computer

—Pipeline

—Shared memory

—Message passing

● Problems are solved in different ways according to the model of parallelism.

PART 1

CATEGORIES OF PARALLEL PROGRAMMING MODELS

2 *Sequential Processing*

Currently most of the well-known programming languages are inherently sequential. Studying these existing models of programming will (hopefully) help in the understanding of the new ones that will be introduced.

> In the *kitchen sink drama* this is where Mum has to perform all the chores by herself following a predetermined pattern. There may be choices to be made but they will always be deterministic choices (e.g. if the glass is clean put it in the cupboard).

.1 CONVENTIONAL LANGUAGES

In languages such as Pascal the normal *flow of control* through a program is that a statement is executed and then control passes to the next one in sequence. This is sometimes called the von Neumann model of programming. The semi-colon separating two Pascal statements can be translated into *pass control from one statement to the next*.

```
begin
      a: = b + c;
      d: = e + f;
      g: = c − e
end
```

In this example there is a block of program statements (delimited by **begin** and **end**). The first statement in the block is an assignment to a variable called **a**. The values associated with the identifiers **b** and **c** are added together and the result stored in the location in memory associated with the identifier **a**. On completion of this statement control passes to the next statement, which is an assignment to the variable **d**. On completion of the assignment to **d** control passes to the next statement, which is an assignment to the variable **g**. The word **end** marks the end of the block and does not need to be separated from the last statement. The block itself can be treated as a statement. A semi-colon after the **end** will serve as a separator between the block and any subsequent statements.

In some languages (such as C) the role of the semi-colon is slightly different: it acts as a *terminator* of statements rather than a *separator*. It still has the same underlying meaning of *go on to the next statement*. Other languages (e.g. Fortran and Basic) rely on the fact there is one statement per line and that unless the statement dictates otherwise the *end of line* character is translated to *go on to the next statement*.

Loops and conditionals do not always pass control to the following statement but control is always passed to a specific statement. At any one time only one statement is being executed and that determines where control passes to next. Consider the simple conditional:

if condition **then** S1 **else** S2;

When this statement is executed the value of the condition is evaluated and depending on the result either statement S1 or S2 will be executed. After that the next statement in the program is executed. Thus for the statement:

if b=1 **then** a:=1 **else** a:=2;

When this **if**-statement is executed the value of the variable **b** is evaluated and depending on the result **a** is assigned the value 1 or 2. After that the next statement in the program is executed. At the time the program was written it was not possible to determine what the value of condition would be (otherwise why use a conditional statement?), but it was certain that if this **if**-statement was executed either:

a:=1
or a:=2

would be executed. The decision as to which would be executed would depend solely on the value of **b**, at this point in the execution of the program.

Many programs spend a great deal of their execution time in a small part of the program that is executed repeatedly. Such repetitions are controlled by a repetition construct. There are many variations on the repetition construct, including:

1. Looping a calculated number of times
2. Looping until a condition is met
3. Looping while a condition holds

Consider the following loop:

```
for i: = 1 to 5 do S1;
S2
```

The statement S1 is executed five times and then the statement S2 is executed. The semantics of most languages forbid the assignment of a value to the control variable (i in this example) during the execution of the loop. It is still possible to predict the actions when the control variable is assigned to, but it is a very dubious programming practice. The control variable is frequently used within such calculations, often as an index to an array. For example, consider the following expression of the multiplication of two 64 by 64 matrices A and B.

```
for r: = 1 to 64 do
    for s: = 1 to 64 do
    begin
        C[r,s]:=0
        for t: = 1 to 64 do
            C[r,s]:=C[r,s]+A[r,t]*B[t,s]
    end
```

Here the loops are nested, but it is simple to determine that the outermost loop will be executed 64 times, and after that control will pass to the next statement in the program. The middle loop will be executed 64×64 times, after each 64 iterations control will pass to the outermost loop for r to be incremented. The innermost loop will be executed $64 \times 64 \times 64$ times; every 64 iterations control will pass to the middle loop for s to be incremented and $C[r,s]$ to be set to zero.

Procedure and function calls also alter the flow of control but again in a predictable hierarchical fashion. When a call is made the address of the next statement is stored and then control is passed to the procedure; when the procedure completes execution control is returned to the saved address. For example:

```
PROCEDURE PrintLine;
BEGIN
  PRINT (---- );
END;
:
BEGIN (*Main program*)
:
x: = 2;
PrintLine;
y: = 3;
:
END
```

In the above fragment of program, after x was assigned the value of 2, the control would pass to the procedure PrintLine and the return address would be stored as the statement assigning to y. Thus, the procedure PrintLine would be executed and when completed control would pass to the stored address and the value 3 would be assigned to y.

Recursive calls result in a number of return addresses becoming stacked up, but the address to return to can always be taken from the top of the stack.

The **goto** statement so shunned by modern-day programmers may be very harmful to structured programming techniques. However, it is always clear to where control is transferred.

2.2 COROUTINES

Coroutines are similar to procedures except control is transferred in a symmetric rather than hierarchical fashion. Programming languages with coroutines available are often said to allow *concurrent programming*. However, it must be remarked that at any one time only one statement is being executed. Control passes between coroutines via a *resume* statement. A coroutine always restarts at the statement after the one that caused it to relinquish control. For example, two coroutines may take the form:

coroutine first	coroutine second
:	:
first.1	*second.1*
:	:
resume second	:
:	resume first
:	:
first.2	*second.2*
:	:
:	resume first
resume second	:
:	:
first.3	*second.3*
:	:

Assuming control is originally with the coroutine first, it will execute the code labelled *first.1*; when first reaches the statement **resume second** it will transfer control to the coroutine second, storing the address of the next statement of first which is where the coroutine will next start, when it is resumed. Second will execute the code labelled *second.1* and when it reaches the statement **resume first** it will transfer control to the coroutine first at its stored address; the address of the next statement in second will be stored as a return address.

Thus the statements will be executed in this order:

:
first.1
:
:
second.1

:
:
first.2
:
:
second.2
:
:
first.3
:

N.B. The statements labelled *second.3* will not be executed, as a result of any of the coroutines shown: a third **resume second** would enable their execution.

Many coroutines can be involved in the exchange of control, but only one of them will have control at a given time. The order in which the statements of the coroutine will be executed are deterministic. The order of execution can be calculated given the values of any variables read in and the coroutine that is first initiated.

In the sequential kitchen sink drama there may be a number of coroutines, say:
   fetching dishes
   washing dishes
   drying dishes
   putting dishes away
Mum (control) may start with the first coroutine (fetching dishes); when there is a sizeable pile Mum will pass control to the washing dishes coroutine, from which she may then pass control back to fetching dishes or onwards to drying them.

A number of programming languages use the concept of coroutines, in particular languages such as Simula and Modula-2.

2.3 SIMULA

The programming language Simula was developed, under the name of Simula 67, by Dahl, Myhrhaug and Nygaard [Birtwhistle et al 1973] while working at Norwegian Computing Centre. Simula is an extension of the programming language Algol 60. Although mainly used as a simulation language it is really a general-purpose programming language, of which simulation is just one application. Most correct Algol 60 programs are also correct Simula programs, as Algol 60 (with some minor exceptions) is a subset of Simula. The extensions include a number of concepts including coroutines.

Simula uses coroutines to create an illusion of parallelism. The language itself is seen as implemented on a sequential processor that can only execute one statement at a time. The body of a coroutine usually has the form:

```
while condition do
begin
    :
    actions;
    :
    resume other coroutines
    :
    actions;
    :
end;
```

the loop body will contain one or more **resume** statements, which will transfer control to similarly structured coroutines. The *condition* will often be TRUE, to represent an always present process. When the execution of the program terminates such coroutines will no longer be resumed. For the system to terminate, one of the coroutines will need to have a condition other than TRUE.

Coroutines are usually created within the body of the main program, by the use of **new**.

```
coroutine1 :-new class1;
coroutine2 :-new class2;
coroutine3 :-new class3;
    :
```

The above would create three new coroutines, coroutine1, coroutine2 and coroutine3; these would be previously defined in the class definitions of class1, class2 and class3 respectively. They could all be of the same class. On the execution of the **new** command control will pass to the coroutine defined. To enable control to be transferred back to the creating process, it is necessary that the new coroutine has a **detach** statement, at a suitable point, that will relinquish control to its creator. The usual place for a **detach** statement is immediately before the main loop of the coroutine.

```
detach;
while condition do
begin
    :
    actions;
    :
    resume other coroutines
    :
    actions;
    :
end;
```

When this coroutine is subsequently resumed it will start at the next statement after the **detach**; in the above example that is with the loop.

4   *MODULA-2*

Modula-2 is the direct descendant of Wirth's programming language Modula [Wirth 1977], which is itself a descendent of Pascal. Major revisions of Modula in the late 1970s led to the development of Modula-2. Mostly Modula-2 is referred to as a successor to Pascal, with the major Pascal errors corrected, but this does ignore the fact that it was via Modula that the facilities for handling concurrency were introduced.

Modula was designed to run on a *naked machine* without any operating system support. It was intended to be a language for programming industrial control and real-time systems. Much of its structure is similar to Pascal, to which the modules with input and output clauses are added. Processes are provided along with **interface modules**, which are like monitors (see Chapter 5).

During the revisions that led to Modula-2 the direct implementation of processes and monitors was removed. Thus the parallelism within Modula-2 is the illusion of coroutines, because of a design decision that implementations would generally run on single processors. Standard modules exist that will allow process creation and monitor-like synchronization; however, because these are not part of the language their implementation cannot be guaranteed.

The main constructs of Modula-2 are procedures and modules: the role of the procedure is similar to the one it takes in most other languages (see earlier in this chapter). Modules are perhaps the most important feature of Modula-2. Modules can either be local or separately compiled. In both cases the visibility of identifiers is controlled by the use of **import** (and in early versions **export**) lists.

Local modules essentially differ from procedures in their tighter control over the scope and visibility of identifiers. Separately compiled modules have a number of additional advantages:

1. Modules can be compiled individually, so when one module is altered only it needs to be recompiled.

2. New programs can be constructed from existing, separately developed modules.

3. Modules help to separate concerns and can be developed independently (maybe even in parallel!).

A Modula-2 coroutine has essentially the same syntax as a procedure. Coroutines are created by changing an existing procedure into a process.

Having thus created a coroutine it will be necessary to transfer control to it and allow it to transfer control to other processes. This transfer of control does not have to be at a fixed place; procedures always start at the beginning, coroutines start where they *left off*.

To use coroutines it is necessary to import procedures from a library module called SYSTEM. In particular the following will be needed:

1. NEWPROCESS—the routine that turns a procedure into a process. NEWPROCESS takes four parameters:
   - The name of a parameterless procedure that is to be turned into a coroutine
   - The address of a region of memory that can be used by this coroutine
   - The size of this region (easily obtained using the standard function SIZE)
   - The name by which this coroutine will be known
2. TRANSFER—The procedure that transfers control to a specified process. TRANSFER takes two parameters:
   - The first parameter saves the state of the current coroutine
   - The second parameter indicates which coroutine now has control, the state of the coroutine been recreated from the information in this parameter

Additionally ADDRESS (formerly known as PROCESS) and ADR are needed for housekeeping.

```
MODULE Example;
FROM SYSTEM IMPORT TRANSFER, NEWPROCESS, ADDRESS, ADR;
FROM InOut IMPORT WriteString, WriteLn;
VAR
Coroutine1,Coroutine2: ADDRESS; (*Coroutines definition*)
I : CARDINAL;
WorkSpace : ARRAY [0..500] OF CARDINAL;
PROCEDURE Susie;
  BEGIN
  LOOP (*forever*)
   WriteString ("Susie to ");
   WriteLn;
   TRANSFER (Coroutine1, Coroutine2);
  END;
END Susie;
BEGIN
  NEWPROCESS (Susie, ADR (WorkSpace), SIZE (WorkSpace), Coroutine1);
  FOR I: = 1 TO 3 DO
   WriteString ("Thomas to ");
   TRANSFER (Coroutine2,Coroutine1);
  END;
END Example.
```

The above program uses two coroutines: one, Coroutine2, is the main program, while the other is based on the procedure Susie; the procedure is turned into Coroutine1 by applying the procedure NEWPROCESS, imported from SYSTEM. The output from the execution of the above program will be:

Thomas to Susie to
Thomas to Susie to
Thomas to Susie to

This shows how control starts with Coroutine2, then passes control to Coroutine1 and goes backwards and forwards between them two more times. The program terminates because Coroutine2 reaches the statement END Example. Coroutine1 only ceases to exist because the program has terminated. A larger program with other initiated coroutines could allow further transfers to Coroutine1.

.5   GUARDED COMMANDS

In the previous section a number of programming constructs have been described. All of these constructs by their nature (i.e. formal or informal semantics) are *deterministic*. The execution of any statement linked by these constructs is uniquely determined by the state of the program variables immediately before the execution of the statement. Deterministic programs are relatively easy to test, using both formal and informal techniques.

Dijkstra [1975] introduces *non-determinism* into sequential programming by the use of guarded commands; thus enabling a better representation for the design and implementation of programs. If the choice of executing A or B is non-deterministic, then not even the most careful study of the internal or external environment should reveal which of them will be executed. Nor is it possible to draw conclusions from previous executions: just because A was chosen the last 87 times does not affect whether or not it is chosen this time.

> If a red ball and a green ball of identical weight and feel were put in a bag and Joe was asked to take one out, which would he choose?

A guarded command consists of a *guard* (a boolean expression), followed by an arrow and then a *guarded list* (i.e. a series of program statements). The guarded list is only eligible for execution when its guard is true (i.e. not to say it will definitely be executed when its guard is true). For example:

$x > y \rightarrow max := x$

In this statement the guard is $x > y$; if the guard is true (i.e. x is greater than y) the variable max **may be** assigned the value of x.

Vending machine examples are widely used to represent non-deterministic behaviour!

e.g. coin→chocolate bar

Here the guard is coin: when coin is true, the statement chocolate bar may be executed.

When a guard is chosen if possible it is *consumed*: thus in the vending machine example the coin will be removed from the slot to the inners of the machine! However, the guard:

$x > y$

cannot be consumed, and so even after this guarded command has been executed x will still be bigger than y (unless either of their values are changed within the guarded list). To summarize, when the chosen guard is executed, the execution may alter values associated with the guard. Testing of guards does not alter the values associated with it.

Sets of guarded commands may be linked by either an *alternative construct* or a *repetitive construct*. The component commands are usually separated by the symbol □. The order in which the commands appear is purely arbitrary (there is no implication of sequencing or priority).

The alternative construct is bracketed by the symbols **if** and **fi** (or open and close brackets).

When control reaches a guarded statement all the guards are evaluated. Then one of the eligible guarded lists is selected (in a non-deterministic manner) and executed. Control will then pass to the next program statement. The program will abort if none of the guards are true. For example:

```
if
    x>y→max: = x
□
    y>x→max: = y
fi
```

In the above example when the value of x is greater than y, the value of x will be assigned to max (as $x > y$ is the only true guard). When the value of y is greater than x the value of y will be assigned to max. If x is equal to y neither of the guards will be true and this will cause the program to abort.

The above example could be rewritten to avoid the possibility of aborting when x and y are equal:

```
if
    x≥y→max: = x
□
    y≥x→max: = y
fi
```

Now if x and y are equal both guards will evaluate to true and a non-deterministic choice will be made between assigning max the value of x and assigning max the value of y. The other cases are as previously explained.

A vending machine example of the alternative construct may be as in the following:

```
if
    coin→tea
    □
    coin→coffee
fi
```

This would describe the action of a rogue vending machine that would accept money and of its own accord decide whether to provide a drink of tea or coffee.

The repetitive construct is bracketed by **do** and **od** (or open and close brackets followed by a star). The guards are repeatedly evaluated and an eligible guard list is executed. Control will pass to the next program statement only when no guard evaluates to true. For example:

```
do
    element1 > element2→
    temp: = element1;
    element1: = element2;
    element2: = temp
    □
    element2 > element3→
    temp: = element2;
    element2: = element3;
    element3: = temp
    □
    element3 > element4→
    temp: = element3;
    element3: = element4;
    element4: = temp
od
```

In the above example a list of four elements is sorted into ascending order. On each iteration the three guards:

```
element1 > element2
element2 > element3
element3 > element4
```

are calculated, taking element1 to be the first element in the current list, element2 to be the second, element3 to be the third and element4 to be the last. Thus information associated with elements may alter after an iteration.

If all the guards are false then the list is in ascending order. If only one guard is true the statements in its guarded list are executed, whereas if two or three guards are true it will be necessary to choose one non-deterministically and execute the statements in its guarded list. Once the statements in a guarded list have been executed the list of elements is reordered and all the guards will have to be recalculated. If the list of elements to be sorted was:

4, 3, 2, 1

on the first iteration of the loop all the guards would be true. The choice of guard will affect which guards are true on the next iteration. On completion the list of elements will be in ascending order whichever guard was originally chosen.

The earlier vending machine example would only dispense a single drink. A more useful vending machine would produce an endless supply of beverages:

```
do
    coin→tea
□
    coin→coffee
□
    no coin→skip
od
```

Unfortunately the nature of the drink is still non-deterministic. However, the **no coin** guard means that at least one guard is always true, so whenever a coin is present this vending machine will deliver a beverage.

Guards may as above consist of a single boolean or may be several conditions linked by the usual boolean operations. For example:

```
do
    coin and tea button→tea
□
    coin and coffee button→coffee
□
    no button→skip
□
    no coin→skip
od
```

Note that the coin is removed from the input (consumed) when the guard that uses it is chosen. Thus if coin is true during one cycle it will be false during the next cycle, unless of course someone inserts another coin.

A final alternative condition is sometimes allowed, that will be executed only if all guards evaluate to false. The earlier example may then be written as:

```
do
    coin→
          (tea button→tea
             □
           coffee button→coffee)
else
    skip
od
```

Note that in this case the presence of a coin causes the system to wait for a button to be pressed.

CHAPTER REVIEW

- In conventional sequential languages a statement is executed and then control passes to the next statement in sequence
- Various constructs exist to alter the sequence of execution, for example:
  - Goto
  - Loops
  - Procedures
  - Coroutines
- Most sequential programs are *deterministic*:
  - that is, the order in which statements are executed is uniquely determined by the state of the program variables
- Guarded commands can be used to introduce *non-determinism* into sequential programs:
  - if two statements are protected by guards both of which are true, there is no way of determining which of the statements will be executed.

3 Array Processing

Processor arrays consist of a number of *identical* processing units all under the control of a common control unit.

> These are the mindless clones in the dishwashing scenario, capable of only doing (or ignoring) the current instruction from the *boss*.
> Another example might be a *keep fit* class where the teacher stands at the front, tells the class to jump in the air and simultaneously all members of the class leave the floor!

Each processing unit has access to its own data items. Thus the same operation can be performed simultaneously on many items of data. In Flynn's terms this is SIMD (single instruction stream–multiple data stream).

Thus a typical system will have an array of P processors and a single control unit whose function it is to direct the processors activities (see Figure 3.1).

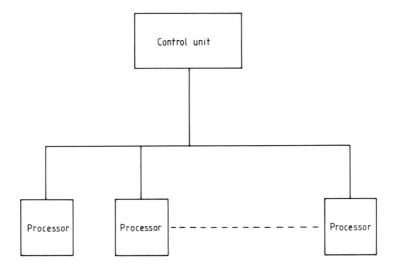

Figure 3.1 A processor array

Processors will also have memory associated with them. The speed of transfer and communication between processors, host and memory will influence the performance capabilities of an architecture [Hockney and Jesshope 1988].

3.1 A PROCESSOR ARRAY

A processor array uses a control unit to broadcast individual instructions to all of the processors in the array. The processors then perform the instruction that was broadcast. The action of the processors is in *lockstep*, that is their actions are synchronized to perform the same instruction using different data; processing takes the same time, for a specific instruction, for each processor.

```
for all i←1 to 64 do
     Answer [i] := B[i] − C[i];
```

In the above example the array **Answer** is set to the difference of the two arrays **B** and **C**. With a 64 processing element processor array the elements B[1] and C[1] can be assigned to the first processing element, the elements B[2] and C[2] can be assigned to the second, . . . and B[64] and C[64] can be assigned to the 64th processing element. The control unit can direct each processing element to take the difference of its **B** and **C** element then store the result in the appropriate element of **Answer**. This has in fact the same effect as executing the following code on a sequential machine:

```
for i←1 to 64 do
     Answer [i] := B[i] − C[i];
```

except this would calculate Answer[1] and then go on to calculate Answer[2] and then Answer[3] . . . and finally Answer[64], whereas the processor array example calculated these values all in one go (i.e. simultaneously or in lockstep).

3.1.1 Timing

If one of the processing elements takes a time T to execute a particular instruction I, then all P of the processing elements that constitute the processor array could together (i.e. P times) execute the same instruction I, on different items of data in the same time (i.e. T). Thus, in theory, the time taken to execute a particular instruction is reduced by $1/P$. In reality there may be an overhead involved in getting the data to the processing elements.

> One mindless clone may take 2 minutes to wash a dinner plate.
> Eight clones would then take 2 minutes to wash eight dinner plates. However,
> if only one clone at a time can fit through the door to the dining room, there
> will be some delay before all are ready to execute the instruction from their
> controller.
> Care will also be needed to avoid arguments over who gets which plate.

Processor arrays are frequently used to execute simple operations, such as addition. If the time taken to add a pair of operands is T seconds, then the time taken to perform P of these operations is also T, on a processor array with P processing elements, and the number of operations per second on the processor array is P/T.

Processors can be enabled (disabled) in any combination, with the result that they execute (or not) the instruction currently broadcast. This is useful for conditionals and when the number of times an operation must be performed is not the same as the number of processors.

> Suppose there were 12 mindless clones but only eight plates on the table; the
> controller would tell four of them to ignore the next series of instructions (by
> going to sleep!).
> The other eight could then fetch themselves a plate.
> The next step might be to check if there was any waste food on the plate and
> only those with such food should follow the next instruction.
> Scrape food into bin.
> All eight clones could then wash their dishes as directed by their boss.
> The remaining four processors can then wake up.

Even with very large arrays of processors it is not always possible to have as many processing elements available as there are processes potentially requiring to be executed at any one point. The time required to execute such large numbers of processors can be readily approximated. If the number of operations required is a direct multiple (M) of the number of processors, then the time to calculate all values is $M \times T$, while if the number of operations is less than P, the time will still be T.

The general case for any number (N) of operations is:

$$\lceil N/P \rceil \times T$$

where $\lceil X \rceil$ is the *ceiling* of X
i.e. X, if X is a whole number
or the next whole number greater than X.

Thus it is possible to compute how long will it take to sum two 1000-element arrays on a variety of processor arrays with varying numbers of processing elements, if the time taken for one processing element to sum two numbers is T seconds. For instance, with:

(i) *100 processors*
$\lceil 1000/100 \rceil \times T = 10 \times T$ seconds.
(ii) *16 384 processors*
$\lceil 1000/16384 \rceil \times T = 1 \times T$ seconds.
(iii) *64 processors*
$\lceil 1000/64 \rceil \times T = 16 \times T$ seconds.

With (i) all the processing elements are in use all the time, whereas with (ii) 15 384 processors are never used. In (iii) all the processing elements are used 15 times for different parts of the array. After computing these sums there will remain another 40 pairs of elements to sum, using 40 processing elements; the remaining 24 will not be used for just this one calculation.

3.1.2 Processors

Processor arrays are usually constructed from very cheap and simple processors (both the Distributed Array Processor and Massively Parallel Processor are based on one-bit processors). The individual processing elements require some way of communicating with each other and with memory. The most common organization for processor arrays is in a two-dimensional array of processing elements with a link between nearest neighbours (Figure 3.2). It is from this layout that the term *processor array* is coined. Sometimes the term *array processor* is used to describe such architectures; unfortunately that term is sometimes used to refer to pipelined

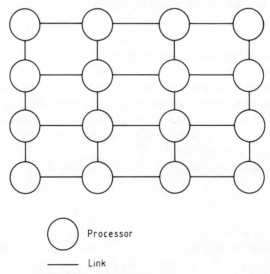

         Processor

         Link

Figure 3.2 *Two-dimensional nearest-neighbour connection (NEWS fashion, i.e. north, east, south, west interconnections)*

systems (see Chapter 4) such as when describing FPS AP 120 B. The term *processor array* is used here to avoid that confusion. Other processor array configurations are possible, for example, pyramids and hypercubes. The plethora of possible interconnections is not just limited to processor arrays: Hockney and Jesshope [1988] discuss such networks for all parallel-type architectures.

Currently the most economical design for a processor array appears to be based on two-dimensional array of one-bit processors with nearest-neighbour interconnection.

.1.3 Memory

As mentioned earlier, each processing element can have associated with it a memory element; this memory is used to hold the data on which the processing element will perform the instruction issued by the controller. These data have to be brought from somewhere and delivered somewhere:

- other processing elements or related memory
- outside the system (host computer)

The ways in which these communicate with each other will greatly affect the efficiency of the machine, but frequently the best communication for one application will not be effective for another.

.1.4 Interprocessor Communication

The ease with which two processing elements can communicate with each other will be determined by the way in which they are interconnected. A processing element that is connected in a ring to other processing elements (Figure 3.3) will be able to readily receive information from the preceding processing element. For instance, if each processing element has just calculated its value of Answer[i] (as described earlier) and then is asked to calculate a new result based on Answer[i−1]:

```
for all i←1 to 64 do
    Result[i]:=Answer[i-1]*B[i];
```

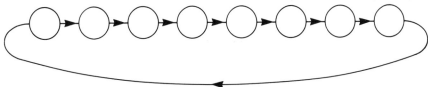

Figure 3.3 *A uni-directional ring*

A ring connection will allow easy transfer of Answer[i-1] from its neighbour.

With this type of calculation it is important that consideration is given to boundary conditions, there are two commom approaches:

1. Special values are put on the boundaries (e.g. Answer[0] which is not computed in the previous calculation may be set to one).

2. Values may be *wrapped round*, thus the nearest neighbours to the first element may be the second and the *last* elements.

Ring connections only allow one-way communication; a nearest-neighbour interconnection allows two-way flow (Figure 3.4). Processing elements that are connected to their nearest neighbour will be able to readily exchange information with these neighbours. This would be useful if having calculated the values of **Result** it was necessary to take a weighted average of the nearest values of **Result**:

```
for all i←1 to 64 do
        Weight[i]: = (Result[i − 1] + 2 × Result[i] + Result[i + 1]);
```

A nearest-neighbour connection will allow easy transfer to the ith processing element of both **Result[i-1]** and **Result[i+1]**.

Both of the above examples of calculating **Result** and **Weight** would have the same effect if they were calculated in a sequential manner; however, the following would not:

```
For all i←1 to 64 do
        Weight [i]: = (Weight [i-1] + 4 × Weight [i] + Weight [i + 1]);
```

In a processor array environment all the new values of **Weight** would be calculated in terms of the old values of **Weight**. So if all the original values of **Weight** (including those on the boundaries) were 1, the new values in **Weight** would be 6.

A similar sequential version might be:

```
for i←1 to 64 do
    Weight [i] : = (Weight [i-1] + 4 × Weight [i] + Weight [i + 1]);
```

Executed sequentially this would result in new values being supplied for **Weight[i-1]** and old values for **Weight[i+1]**. So if all the original values of **Weight** (including those on the boundaries) were 1, the new values in **Weight** would be an increasing series of values:

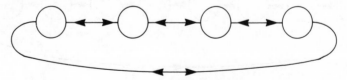

Figure 3.4 *A bi-directional ring*

[6, 11, 16, 21, . . ., 316, 321]

Quite a different answer from the processor array version!

Communication may not always be on a nearest neighbour basis, but may still be fairly regular, e.g.:

```
for all i←1 to 64 do
    Weight [i] : = (Weight [i-4] + 4 × Weight [i] + Weight [i + 4]);
```

Such an algorithm if implemented on a nearest-neighbour architecture would require information to be passed via intermediate processing elements or via some other memory. A *clever* compiler or *judicious* programming could map those processes that communicate on to adjacent processing elements. The first processing element could calculate **Weight**[1], the second **Weight**[5], the third **Weight**[9], etc. Once again care must be taken at the boundaries.

Not all algorithms are so regular; for example, Poisson solvers are better suited to interconnections based on Stone's perfect shuffle (Figure 3.5). This is a prime example of an interconnection structure being chosen because it reflects a real-world solution to a problem.

Grosch [1979] has suggested an interconnection that is based on a combination of the perfect shuffle and nearest-neighbour interconnections that is particularly well suited for the use with Buneman's algorithm for the Poisson problem.

It is not necessary for there to be direct interprocessor communication as described above: the Illiac IV used an interconnection network to link all processing elements. Other arrangements are possible where processing elements can cluster round memory modules, such as in hierarchically organized machines [Mead and Conway 1980] where all the processing elements in a particular cluster can readily communicate, but communication in between different clusters can be much more time consuming. See Figure 3.6.

The Connection Machine provides *programmable connections* between any two processors; these connections can change *dynamically* during the execution of a program.

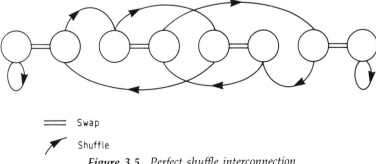

═══ Swap

⟋ Shuffle

Figure 3.5 Perfect shuffle interconnection

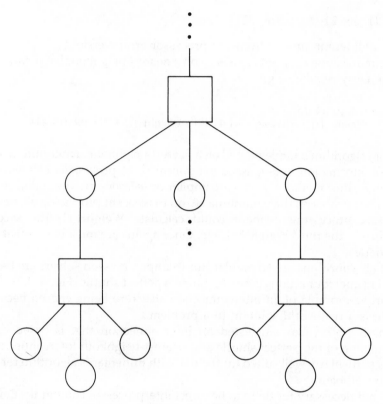

Figure 3.6 *Clusters*

3.1.5 External Communication

Processor arrays are only really well suited to a small set of calculations and for this reason are usually attached to a *host* computer that will download suitable sub-programs onto the processor array. This means that there will be a need for communication between the host computer and the processor array. The processor array may run at the same time as the host computer (i.e. in parallel) or the host may suspend while the processor array executes (i.e. sequentially).

A delay in passing information to the processor array or receiving it back may well have a negative effect on the performance of the overall system.

The Distributed Array Processor is treated by the host processor as **memory** and the communication costs are in that case the same as for any other memory transfers by the host.

The other approach is to have a number of input/output channels along a row of the array, which allows rows of information to be shifted from the processor array to the **host**. Shifting information from one row to the next can be used to transmit results in every processing element to the **host**.

3.2 PROCESSOR ARRAY ARCHITECTURES

A great problem in programming for a processor array is that it is necessary to be aware of the underlying hardware architecture, if efficient (or even *runnable*) programs are to be produced. The differences between the architectures even under the heading of processor arrays is great and in this section three architectures that can be called processor arrays are briefly described:

1. Connection Machine
2. DAP
3. MPP

Other examples can be found in Hockney and Jesshope [1988].

3.2.1 The Connection Machine

The Connection Machine was developed at MIT primarily for use as a parallel artificial intelligence engine [Hillis 1985]. Thinking Machine Corporation market versions of this machine. The full Connection Machine is intended to be a 1024×1024 array of processing elements linked in to a 14-cube (i.e. a hypercube apparently linked in 14 dimensions). The CM-1 version is based on 64×1024 one-bit processing elements. Each of the processing elements has associated with it 4K bits of memory. It is possible to map 64 virtual processors to each of the real processors to emulate the full machine. This would of course limit the amount of memory available to the processors (effectively dividing by 64).

The individual processing elements can be connected together using the programmable connection network. These connections form *active data structures* that can be manipulated by instructions from the host computer, which has access to the processors' memory via a data bus. Instructions from the host (and data returning to it) are buffered by the control unit.

The newer CM-2 version adds several features to the CM-1 including the addition of floating-point chips, thus answering the needs of more applications.

3.2.2 The DAP

The DAP (Distributed Array Processor) was developed by ICL during the 1970s. Development work and marketing is now undertaken by Active Memory Technology Ltd (AMT). Thus, confusingly, the DAP is sometimes referred to as the ICL DAP and elsewhere as the AMT DAP.

The DAP is based on a 64×64 array of one-bit processing elements (there is a mini-DAP with 16×16 processing elements). Associated with each processing element is 4K bits of memory. Processing elements are linked to their nearest neighbours in a NEWS fashion (i.e. north, east, west and south connections; see Figure 3.2), with a wrap-around at the edge of the array (e.g. north of the top row is the bottom row). The one-bit processing elements can be used to provide arithmetic of any precision. Eight 64-bit registers are connected to row and column highways to select (or send) data from (to) all processors in a row or column (Figure 3.7). The transfer to the processors in a row (or column) is simultaneous. When data are to be output each processor may add extra information, as it passes the output back to the highway.

The host processor of the DAP can treat the whole of the DAP (processing elements and internal memory) as its own memory, which can be addressed as part of its own address space; thus the DAP can be viewed as an array of processors that have been set above and added to a memory bank of a sequential computer. This configuration allows essentially sequential parts of a program to be executed by the host while those well suited to the processor array are executed there. The host of course can be multiprogrammed, which may be a disadvantage, if this means that the extra performance of the DAP is negated by a wait for the operating system's attention. The configuration could in theory be used to multiprogram the DAP, but this may again have a negative effect on performance.

3.2.3 The MPP

Goodyear Aerospace Corporation developed the Massively Parallel Processor (MPP) under a contract from NASA, at about the same time as the DAP was under development in the UK. Many of the concepts for the MPP are

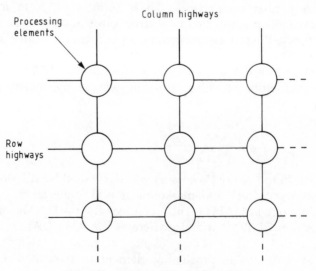

FIG. 3.7 Column and row highways

similar to those for the DAP, although the MPP was designed to meet a need for an ultra high-speed image processing system; like the DAP it is flexible and able to handle a wide range of problems.

The MPP is based on a two-dimensional array of 128×128 one-bit processing elements, with four spare columns to by-pass faulty hardware. Data are stored in 1024 128×128 one-bit memory *planes*, and with 35 processing planes this makes the **array unit** (ARU). For example, an array of 16 384 pixels with N bits per pixel will be stored on N planes of the array unit. The processing elements of the MPP are linked to each other under the nearest-neighbour principle. As with the DAP these are the four square neighbours NEWS. Unlike the DAP, there is no wrap-around at the edge of the array.

Extra registers and grid links allow input and output across the rows of the MPP. Data are shifted across the rows, so 128 operations are required to shift out the whole of an array. This shifting does not prevent other operations being performed on the data stored in the processing elements, because it is done in a special S-plane and then transferred *en masse* to the appropriate memory plane (or vice versa for output). A *data interface* is used to allow the host computer to pass data to and from the processor array. A *control interface* is used to allow the host computer to pass instructions to the processor array.

.2.4 Languages

The most usual approach to developing languages for processor arrays is to adapt a sequential language; sometimes new languages are designed and there are hopes of designing a general array-processing language.

Much of the work of processor arrays is the classical *number crunching*. For this reason it is not surprising to find that there are languages that are variations on Fortran. The other area for which processor arrays are often used in array processing is image processing and this has led to variants of LISP. Other languages that have been considered for extensions are Algol and Pascal.

.3 *DAP-FORTRAN*

Currently the most widely used scientific language is Fortran. This wide acceptance of Fortran by the numerical computation community was the basis for the development of a number of variations on Fortran for a variety of different processor arrays, since the manufacturers were marketing their machines towards this scientific market. So the originators of DAP chose as the first high-level language for their machine a variation on Fortran.

DAP-Fortran programs are only suitable for execution on the DAP (or a simulator) as special operations are introduced that are directly mappable to the hardware. Thus programs are not portable beyond the DAP community, but the programmer is able to take advantage of the hardware without having to become involved in low-level programming.

The default size of arrays in DAP-Fortran is chosen to match the number of processing elements. Thus vectors can have 64 elements and matrices can have 4096 elements (i.e. 64×64).

```
INTEGER V(), W(), X()
```

The above would define three integer vectors each with 64 elements. The statement:

```
V = W + X
```

would sum the two vectors W and X, depositing the result in V. The statement:

```
V = W × X
```

would give an element-by-element multiplication of W and X leaving the result in V, not a vector multiplication.

```
INTEGER VM(,), WM(,), XM(,)
```

The above would define three integer matrices each with 64×64 elements. The statement:

```
VM = WM + XM
```

would sum the two matrices *WM* and *XM*, depositing the result in *VM*. The statement:

```
VM = WM × XM
```

would give an element-by-element multiplication of *WM* and *XM* leaving the result in *VM*, not a matrix multiplication

Up to seven dimensions are permitted; only the first two can take the default values of 64. Other values than 64 can be declared in any dimension.

```
REAL SMALL(2,2),BIG(,,10,15,20,25,30)
```

The above will define a matrix **SMALL** with 2×2 (i.e. 4) real elements and an array **BIG** with $64 \times 64 \times 10 \times 15 \times 20 \times 25 \times 30$ (i.e. $10\,000\,000\,000$) real elements.

Arrays can be declared to be logical, character and double precision as well as real and integers. Scalar values can be treated as arrays:

V + 5

this would add the value 5 to each element of the vector **V**.

VM.GT.0

will produce a 64×64 boolean matrix, with elements set to true corresponding to all elements of **VM** >0; all other elements will be set to false.

Vectors can also be expanded but it is necessary that the programmer indicates whether this is by row or by column.

MATC (V)

will produce a 64×64 matrix with identical columns.

MATR (VM(,5))

will produce a 64×64 matrix with identical rows.

Arrays can be masked to allow assignments to only certain elements. Logical arrays are defined to enable this:

LOGICAL VL()

could be used as a mask for the vectors **V**, **W** and **X**, declared above.

W(VL) = X + 5

would update those elements of **W** corresponding to true values in **VL** to the appropriate value in **X** incremented by 5. The selection must be done on the left-hand side of the assignment; selection on the right-hand side is used only to reduce rank.

The DAP has the ability to readily shift elements. Functions are available for shifting a number of places, but single position shifts can be achieved using the + or − symbols in the first or second dimension.

V(+)   shifts V one place to the left
V(−)   shifts V one place to the right
VM(+,) shifts V one place to the north
VM(−,) shifts V one place to the south
VM(,+) shifts V one place to the west
VM(,−) shifts V one place to the east

Planar geometry is the default, but the GEOMETRY statement can be used to set either planar or cyclic geometry. The functions all take the form of four-lettered function names starting with SH. The third letter indicates direction (L, R, N, E, W or S) and the fourth the geometry (C or P). The arguments to the function are the array's name and the number of places to be shifted.

```
SHNC(VM,2)
```

will shift the matrix **VM** two positions north; those elements falling off the top of the matrix will reappear at the bottom.

```
SHRP(W,4)
```

will shift the vector **W** right four places; the four leftmost places will be filled with zeros, and the four rightmost values will be lost.

A number of other functions are available: standard functions are made polymorphic and special array functions provided, for example, SUM that adds over rows and columns.

3.3.1   Fortran

DAP-Fortran was developed because of the demand for Fortran; however, it is not suited to programming other processor arrays and so also prohibits the porting of programs. To meet both these needs the designers of Fortran 77 considered including array operations as a feature of the language; however, they were discarded, with a recommendation they be included in the next standard, which is now the case. Many of the features for the array operations in the new standard are similar to those of the architecture-specific versions of Fortran; in particular, the designers have obviously been influenced by DAP-Fortran.

Arrays are treated as fundamental data objects. Up to seven dimensions are allowed for arrays which are notionally rectangular. The size of an array can be fixed explicitly, inherited as an argument to a procedure or determined at run time. Bounds do not have to start at 1 (or 0) and so can be represented by a range (e.g. 3:33). As with DAP-Fortran an array reference without subscripts implies the whole array and individual elements and sub-arrays can be chosen by using subscripts, which themselves may be arrays. Arrays can be passed both to user-defined procedures but also to the inbuilt functions, for example the polymorphic SIN will take a REAL and return a REAL, or take a REAL array and return a REAL array. A number of array-specific functions will also be available (e.g. MERGE and REPLICATE).

4 *ACTUS*

The parallel language Actus was developed [Perrott 1987] to enable the programmers of processor arrays and pipelines to utilize recognized software engineering techniques and practices. Actus allows the programmer to represent the natural parallelism within a problem and places the burden of exploiting the parallelism on to the compiler for the particular architecture. The compiler does not need to become involved in the complexities of detecting parallelism (see Chapter 10), only in exploiting the parallelism that the programmer has already highlighted.

Actus is based on Pascal and maintains the basic structure (including the basic syntax and semantics for statements and data types).

A feature that separates Actus from Fortran is that when array data structures are declared the maximum extent of the parallelism is also declared. This extent can be altered within the program by language statements or constructs. Within the declaration of dimensions of arrays sequential dots (..) are used to indicate conventional arrays, e.g.

aa : **array** [1..m, 1..n] **of** real;

indicates an array aa that can not be handled in parallel.

bb : **array** [**1:m, 1..n**] **of** real;

the array bb has a declared extent of parallelism **m** that is associated with its first dimension. **m** elements can be manipulated at one time, with this array. Thus the *j*th column of bb is specified as:

bb[1:m, j]

and all of the elements of the column can be simultaneously involved in operations.

cc : **array** [1..m, 1:n] **of** real;

specifies that the array cc has a declared extent of parallelism **n** that is associated with its second dimension. **n** elements can be manipulated at one time, with this array. Thus the *i*th row of cc is specified as:

cc[i, 1:n]

and all of the elements of the row can be simultaneously involved in operations.

Early versions limited the parallelism to one dimension, but arrays can now have any combination of parallel and scalar dimensions, e.g.

```
seqquad : array [1..w, 1..x, 1..y, 1..z] of real;
parquad : array [1:w, 1:x, 1:y, 1:z] of boolean;
mixquad : array [1..w, 1:x, 1..y, 1:z] of integer;
```

are possible four-dimensional arrays: seqquad is scalar, parquad can have operations applied in parallel to all elements, mixquad may be treated as parallel in its second and fourth dimensions but is scalar for the first and third. The range of arrays need not be contiguous or regular; index sets can be declared to represent any ranges required. Indeed index sets can be combined by any of the usual set operations.

The context within which an array is used dictates the extent of parallelism. This extent must be less than or equal to the extent of parallelism for all the arrays used within the operation. The language requires that the extent of parallelism is consistent for all arrays used within an operation. Scalar subexpressions are expanded to the extent of parallelism required by the expression. Thus:

```
bb[1:m, j] + 2
```

will add the scalar value 2 to each element in the jth column of bb, while:

```
bb[3:6, k] - bb[3:6, i]
```

will subtract from the values of the four specified elements of column k the value of the four elements from column i, assuming the indexes are all within valid ranges, otherwise there would be a compile or run time error.

The **shift** operation is used when selecting elements from dissimilar ranges, while **rotate** does a wrap-round shift in the range specified.

The # symbol is used as a mask, it is set by either a conditional, e.g.

```
while bb[3:6, k] <0 do
    cc[j, #] := 0;
```

would zeroize cc[j,3] if bb[3,k] was zero; similarly if bb[4,k], bb[5,k] or bb[6,k] were zero then cc[j,4], cc[j,5] or cc[j,6] would respectively be zeroized. The **within** statement provides a band within which # is true.

Procedures and functions take the same role as in Pascal, scope rules and the parameter passing mechanism are made to cover extents of parallelism in the same way as other variables. The extent of parallelism of local variables cannot be altered by a procedure or function call. The extent of parallelism of the parallel variables in the actual parameter list must be compatible with that in the formal parameter list.

Standard functions (such as COS) are extended to apply to whole arrays (returning whole arrays). New functions that are array specific are introduced, for example SUM that returns a single result, that is the sum of all the elements in the array to which the function is applied.

Actus allows the user to program processor array types of operations without any need to know details of the target architecture. Additionally these facilities are based within the well-known block-structured language Pascal.

5 CMLISP

CmLisp (Connection Machine Lisp) is an extension of Common Lisp, specifically designed to support the parallel operations of the Connection Machine. Lisp was chosen for a number of reasons as the base for the Connection Machine's language: a primary reason must be that the machine was originally designed for use by the Artificial Intelligence community, in which Lisp is the dominant programming language.

Control flow in CmLisp follows the normal serial Lisp approach. Parallelism is achieved by allowing simultaneous execution of operations across a large data structure. CmLisp allows both processor array type operations and apparently parallel *different* operations, the latter been mapped onto several processor array type operations.

CmLisp makes use of the DEFSTRUCT construct, which was added to Common Lisp to allow the definition of data structures. For example, a data structure for a person may have three components: name, age and weight.

```
(DEFSTRUCT (PERSON)
      NAME
      AGE
      WEIGHT)
```

Evaluation of this defines a number of functions, including:

MAKE-PERSON

this creates a new instance of PERSON.

NAME, AGE and WEIGHT

these three functions are used to access the components of any PERSON structure.

COPY-PERSON

creates a new copy of PERSON with the same components as the original.

PERSON-P

tests if a *given* object is a person.

These are just some of the facets of the DEFSTRUCT mechanism. CmLisp adds a feature to DEFSTRUCT that allows the programmer to specify that all structures of a particular type are to be stored on the connection Machine.

```
(DEFSTRUCT (PERSON : CM)
    NAME
    AGE
    WEIGHT)
```

This causes MAKE-PERSON to store new PERSON structures on the Connection Machine. The other functions work exactly as in Common Lisp.

All parallel operations in CmLisp involve a simple data structure called a **xector**. This includes operations on data structures allocated to the Connection Machine via DEFSTRUCT. A xector can be considered as a set of processors, each containing a value. The xector is meant as an abstraction and so is not defined in terms of processors, but in terms of a domain, a range and a mapping between them. The domain provides an index to the xector, the range provides the value, and the mapping of an index onto a value is an element. A simple example of a xector will map the symbols SEA, SAND and SURF on to the symbols BLUE, YELLOW and WHITE respectively:

{SEA→BLUE SAND→YELLOW SURF→WHITE}

Hillis [1985] introduces a number of special forms of the xector, including the mapping of each index on to itself, indexes starting from 0 and all indexes mapping onto a single value. The latter is represented as:

{→4}

if the single value is 4.

The SETQ function can be used to create a symbol that takes the value of a xector. A function XREF is used to obtain the value of an index of a xector; XSET is used to change this value. A number of functions are available to create Lisp objects from xectors and vice versa.

The alpha notation in CmLisp is used to create a constant xector of its argument. For example,

$\alpha 4 = > \{→4\}$

produces a xector with a constant value of 4. As does the following:

$\alpha (+13) = > \{→4\}$

A xector of functions is applied by mapping the xector across its arguments, returning a xector of the individual results. For example, a xector of the plus function can be applied to two xectors:

$\alpha +'$ {age→2 weight→25} '{age→7 weight→35}
    => {age→9 weight→60}

A xector can be created from any Common Lisp function.

When an index does not occur in all elements it is ignored, for example:

α CONS ' {age→2} '{age→7 weight→35}
    => {age→9}

The alpha operation can be factored over its components; this, however, is not always necessary as some components may already be parallel, so Hillis introduces another symbol, ●, that cancels the effect of the α.

The beta operation is used to reduce portions of xectors and associate the results with other indices. The simplest case is where a xector is reduced to a single value, for example:

$\beta +'$ {age→7 weight→35} => 42

The more general form of the beta operation takes a combining function and two xectors. The first xector provides the values for the resulting xector and the second the indexes for the result. The combining function is used to reduce colliding values to a single value.

$\beta +'$ {1→1 2→2 3→3} {A→A B→B B→B}
    => {A→1 B→5}

If no colliding function is supplied any collision results in an error.

CmLisp can be treated as an abstraction of the Connection Machine, the alpha operators representing the processors, the beta operators the routers of information to processors and the xectors as the contents of the memory cells.

---

6   *CHAPTER REVIEW*

- In a processor array all processors execute the same instruction at the same time
- Each processor has its own data, often supplied to the processor array as an *array*
  - Thus the same instruction can be applied to every element of an array
- Processors can be *masked* to stop an instruction being applied to some member of an array.

4 *Pipeline Processing*

The concept of a *pipeline* is not novel to computing: many factories use the pipeline principle. The name 'pipeline' is derived from the petroleum industry, where a series of hydrocarbon products are pumped through a physical pipeline.

A bakery may be seen as an industry that uses a pipelined approach, where a number of *stations* are linked by a conveyor belt. The first station may continuously mix the dough and put chunks of it (one after the other) on a conveyor belt. The chunks pass on to the proving stage, then on to kneading, on to the second proving stage, into the oven and out on to the cooler. There is no need during processing for the loaf to ever leave the conveyor or the conveyor to be empty.
Car manufacturing is another popular example.

A task can be divided into a number (N) of sequential processes; these N processes can be executed one after another on a single processor or they can be allocated to N different processors. A task which is well suited to pipelining is based on the assumption that one process relies on receiving results computed by the previous process, and the results of the current process are to be used by the next process.

The washing-up scenario is well suited to pipeline processing because the work that is required to be done can readily be divided into tasks: clearing, washing, drying, etc. The washing task relies on receiving an input from the clearing process and the output from the washing is an input to the drying process.

Each process can then be allocated to a separate processor. Having thus allocated the processes, a single execution of the task would result in only one processor being active at a time. The other processors would all either have completed their processing or be waiting for input from earlier processes.

> Consider the case when there is only one plate to be washed. Most of the family would spend a lot of time waiting for their opportunity to *process* the plate. It would be much easier all round if Susie did all of the chore.

If the task were to be executed many times, then more of the processors could be used in parallel, by allowing the second processor to be working on the *i*th task while the first works on the (*i*+1)th and the third processor works on the (*i*-1)th task, etc. (Figure 4.1).

The time taken to execute a single task on a pipeline processor will be similar to the time taken to execute on a single processor. Indeed, if there is an overhead involved in passing information to the next processor the pipeline time may be greater. However, if a large number of tasks are to be executed on an *N*-processor pipeline then the time will approach $1/N$ of the sequential time (assuming that each process takes an equal amount of time).

4.1 A PIPELINE PROCESSOR

There is perhaps no such thing as a general pipeline processor but in this section general principles will be introduced. The pipelines described here

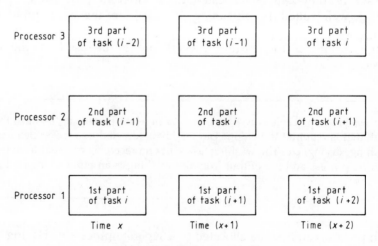

Figure 4.1 *Tasks in a pipeline*

are essentially one-dimensional; the concept can, however, be generalized to any number of dimensions. These general pipelines are sometimes called *systolic arrays* (see Section 4.7)

There are many similarities between the designs of processor arrays and pipeline processors. Confusion sometimes arises because pipeline processors are sometimes referred to as vector processors. The problem is made worse by some manufacturers producing machines that work in a pipeline fashion and calling them array processors. However, the choice of such a name is justified because pipeline processors are particularly well suited to the computation of certain types of array operations.

> Here the confusion is (hopefully) avoided by the use of the term *pipeline processors* to describe machines based on the principle of information flowing along a pipe, while the term *processor array* is used to describe processors that simultaneously execute the same instruction.

Consider the following piece of pseudo-code:

```
for i←1 to 64 do
begin
        A[i]:=B[i]+C[i];
        D[i]:=A[i]+E[i];
        F[i]:=D[i]+G[i]
end
```

In the above the array **F** is set to the sum of arrays **B**, **C**, **E** and **G**. Additionally, array **A** is set to the sum of **B** and **C**, and array **D** is set to the sum of arrays **A** and **E**. A simple pipleline can be envisaged that would produce these results (Figure 4.2).

In this example the first processor contains the values of the array **C**, the second processor contains the values of the array **E**, the third processor contains the values of the array **G**. The first processor is initiated when it

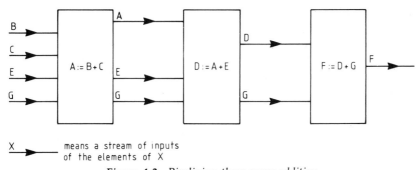

X ———▶ means a stream of inputs of the elements of X

Figure 4.2 *Pipelining three-array addition*

receives the value of B[1], which it adds to its value of C[1], stores in A[1] and passes this result on to the second processor. This action is deemed to take one cycle (or time unit).

Receiving the value of A[1] initiates the action of the second processor. The value of A[1] received is added to the processor's value for E[1], the result is stored in D[1] and passed onto the third processor. During this cycle the first processor will have received the value of B[2] and have calculated A[2]. The third processor will be idle because it has not sufficient values to begin computation (for the same reason both the second and third processors were idle during the first cycle).

During the third cycle all three processors will be active. The first processor will receive the value of B[3] and calculate A[3]. The second processor will receive the value of A[2] and calculate D[2]. The third processor will receive the value of D[1] and calculate F[1].

For the next 61 cycles all the processors will be busy. After the total execution of 64 cycles there will be no new values for the first processor to calculate, as on 64th cycle A[64] was calculated, completing the calculation of values of A that were required. Thus in the 65th cycle the first processor will be idle, the second processor having received the value for A[64] will calculate D[64], while the third processor uses the value received for D[63] to calculate the value of F[63].

In the 66th cycle the first and second processor will be idle. The third processor uses the value received for D[64] to calculate the value of F[64]. On completion of this cycle all the statements required by the loop will have been executed.

Using three pipelined processors the total time taken to execute this loop is 66 time units, where one set of addition of two array elements and their assisgnment to a third will take one time unit. On a single processor then the computation would take 3×64 (192) time units. Of course a processor array with 64 processors would only take 3 time units, if the processors were of the same power.

4.2 PIPE PRIMING

The previous example of adding arrays contains times when some of the processors were idle, as they were unable to start their work because the values they required were not available or they had calculated all the values that they were required to.

In that example during the first cycle both the second and third processors were idle, because they were waiting for their initial values to be provided. Similarly in the second cycle the third processor is still idle. It is only on the third cycle that all processors are busy. The first two cycles are used to *prime* the pipeline. After the time taken

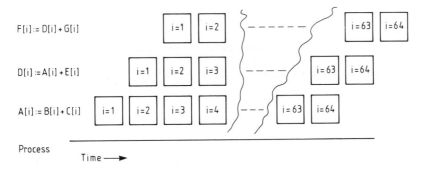

Figure 4.3 *Timing the pipelined addition of three arrays*

to prime the pipeline all processors are busy, until the last two cycles, when the final results have to be *flushed* out of the pipeline. Figure 4.3 shows a timing history of the use of processors within this pipeline computation. Figure 4.4 shows a similar timing diagram for a computation with six stages.

It can be seen that the pipeline priming time for this particular computation is longer. However, this is counterbalanced by the fact that the six stages in the pipeline mean that the overall computation speed is six times that of a sequential representation. The time taken to prime a pipeline is equal to the time (T) taken for one stage of the pipeline to be executed multiplied by the number of stages within the pipeline. Once the pipeline is primed a new result can be produced in the time taken by one stage (i.e. T). Thus the pipe priming time is an overhead of using the pipe: it has to be paid each time the pipeline is used.

A pipeline with three processors each taking T seconds to execute, will take $3 \times T$ seconds to produce the first result, but after that new results will be produced every T seconds; see Table 4.1

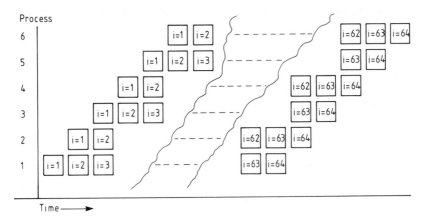

Figure 4.4 *Priming a six-process pipeline*

Table 4.1 *Time per result for a three-processor pipeline*

Three processor pipeline		
Number of results required	**Overall time**	**Time per result**
1	$3 \times T$	$3 \times T$
2	$4 \times T$	$2 \times T$
3	$5 \times T$	$1.6 \times T$
4	$6 \times T$	$1.5 \times T$
5	$7 \times T$	$1.4 \times T$
6	$8 \times T$	$1.33 \times T$
$\vdots$		
$\vdots$		
64	$66 \times T$	$\approx 1.0 \times T$

4.3 CLASSIFICATION OF PIPELINE PROCESSORS

Handler [1982] identifies three different logical levels of pipelining, according to the complexity of the processes:

1. Arithmetic pipelining (i.e. *word level*)

2. Instruction pipelining (i.e. *instruction level*)

3. Macro-pipelining (i.e. *program level*)

Arithmetic pipelining is used to describe the segmentation of the arithmetic operations, so that separate processors are responsible for different parts of the operation. Instruction pipelining can overlap the execution of the current instruction, with the storing of the result of the previous instruction and the decoding of the next.

Instruction pipelining is now widely used; RISC (Reduced Instruction Set Computers) achieve high performance by using the pipeline principle. Although not strictly relevant to parallel programming models, a short introduction to this area is presented as it illustrates some of the difficulties involved in using pipelines.

Macro-pipelining is used to describe the situation where a single data stream passes through a cascade of processors: each processor is programmed to perform a particular task (the task may change every cycle). Macro and arithmetic pipelining are both used in parallel processing environments and are discussed in more detail in the following sections.

4 ARITHMETIC PIPELINE

The term 'arithmetic' pipeline is used here to describe the situations in which arithmetic operations are segmented, and the segments are executed on separate processors. Consider the multiplication of two floating-point numbers. This can be considered in four parts:

1. Addition of exponents
2. Multiplication of mantissas
3. Normalization of the result
4. Rounding where necessary

These parts can be allocated to separate processors within a pipeline (Figure 4.5).

A simple example of the use of this arithmetic pipeline would be the multiplication of:

$7.5\,E\,3 \times 2.1\,E\,4$

Adding exponents gives 7
Multiplication of the mantissas gives 15.75
Normalization will give $1.575\,E\,8$
Rounding may be necessary, for instance if only two significant digits were required, then the result would be:

$1.6\,E\,8$

The addition of floating-point numbers can also be segmentized. Both operands will require mormalizing, before the addition can take place and the result will need normalizing and rounding.
Thus:

$7.5\,E\,3 + 2.1\,E\,4$

would require both components to have the same exponent, e.g.:

$7.5\,E\,3 + 21.0\,E\,3$

giving:

$28.5\,E\,3$

which would be normalized to:

$2.85\,E\,4$

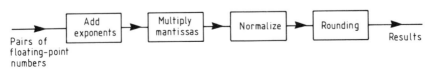

Figure 4.5 *Multiplication pipeline*

Stone (1987) presents a number of ways in which arithmetic operations can be pipelined. When arithmetic is pipelined the way in which it is achieved is (almost) always a feature of the architecture. The user needs to be aware of the length of the pipe, whether the pipes are dedicated to a single operation on a specific data type and if there are a number of pipes that provide different operations that can themselves be multiprocessed. It should not be necessary to be aware of what happens in different segments.

A pipeline processor is said to be *unifunctional* if it is dedicated to a single function. A *multifunctional* pipeline is capable of performing different operations. This can be achieved by changing the task of each processor or interconnecting different stages of the pipeline. The complexity of the change will dictate whether the pipe needs to be flushed or if pipelining can continue uninterrupted over the change of operation.

When the pipeline configuration remains unaltered it is said to be *static*, as opposed to a *dynamic* configuration that allows interconnection of different stages within the pipeline. Static pipelines require much less overheads in control and sequencing.

Arithmetic pipelines usually perform operations on either scalars or vectors. Scalar pipelines are employed on the execution of arithmetic operations on scalars that are within a loop. The loop ensures that the operation is repeated a number of times and so the overhead involved in using the scalar pipeline (including pipe priming time) is worth incurring. Vector pipelines are designed to handle operations on vectors, in particular vector arithmetic. Machines incorporating vector pipelines are often called vector processors.

4.5 INSTRUCTION PIPELINE

A widely used example of pipelining is the instruction execution sequence, which can be divided into a number of processes. For instance, the following four processes can be isolated: *fetch, decode, execute* and *store*. With real architectures there may be more stages in the pipeline. Each process can be performed on a specially designed unit, and having completed its processing can initiate the next process by passing on its results (Figure 4.6).

If the hardware is designed so that each unit takes T seconds to perform its process, a single task will be completed in $4 \times T$ seconds. If a series of instructions are to be executed this pipeline will be able to

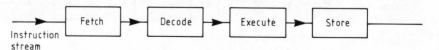

Figure 4.6 *A simple instruction pipeline*

approach an execution speed of one instruction completed every *T* seconds. Indeed, once the pipeline is *primed*, instructions will be completed every *T* seconds.

Consider the following piece of (silly) pseudo assembly code:

```
LDA   A   FIRST      :instruction 1
LDA   B   SECOND     :instruction 2
ADD   A   THIRD      :instruction 3
ADD   B   FOURTH     :instruction 4
ST    A   ANSWER1    :instruction 5
ST    B   ANSWER2    :instruction 6
```

During the first cycle the *fetch* processor fetches instruction 1; all other processors are idle. In the second cycle instruction 2 is fetched while the first instruction is decoded. In the third cycle instruction 3 is fetched, while the second instruction is decoded and the value of FIRST is calculated. At the fourth cycle the pipeline is fully primed and all processors are busy; by the end of this cycle the first instruction will have finished. Similarly the second instruction will be completed at the end of the fifth cycle, the third at the end of the fifth cycle, etc.

What will happen when an instruction that is decoded turns out to be a branch? The sequence described above will lead to instructions that are not going to be needed being fetched and decoded, and when it is realized that the instruction is in fact a jump, the pipeline will have to be flushed, and the instructions at the address jumped to will have to be fetched and decoded. Branches are usually conditional and even if it is possible at the time an instruction is fetched to determine that there is potentially a change in the flow of control, there is then a choice of which set of instructions to subsequently follow. Research may indicate that a particular branch usually occurs, while another type rarely does. The compiler writer (or whoever) may use this information to determine which path is likely to be taken and so fetch and decode the relevant instructions, hopefully minimizing the number of times the pipe will need to be flushed. However, by their nature it is expected that sometimes the other choice will be made (otherwise why is there a branch?) and in this case the pipe will have to be flushed. One approach that is sometimes taken is to have two pipelines: when the one in use recognizes a branch it initiates the other pipe to fetch and decode the instructions that may be branched to while it continues with the statements that will be executed if the branch fails. Of course successive branches will still create problems.

Problems may also arise if a value stored in one instruction is fetched in the next instruction. However, this is not common in compiled code and most assembler programmers would use the value already in the register (or wherever).

4.6 *MACRO-PIPELINING*

Two separate views can be taken of macro-pipelining:

1. A number of similar programmable processors are linked together so that information can only flow in one direction. Usually such architectures are considered to be general purpose (or at least capable of use for a class of problems).

2. A number of dissimilar dedicated processors are linked together so that information flows in one direction. The processors of the pipeline are provided to solve particular *segments* of a problem. It is possible for a *processor* of the pipeline to be composed itself of a number of parallel processors or to be specially fabricated for this problem. Such an architecture is dedicated to the solution of a specific problem.

The former, although offering an interesting architectural model, is rarely realized, probably because it is essentially a special case of the message-passing architectures, and if this model is required it can easily be achieved using message-passing processors (such as the transputers; see Chapter 6). Equally there are no specific programming models for this model of parallelism.

4.6.1 Dedicated Macro-pipelining

This section refers to a possible future role of the pipeline model, whereas the preceding sections have all described pipelining as it is currently used.

A variety of computational problems require different computational models at stages in their computations, for example a vision problem may require fine-grain parallelism while detecting edges but a coarse grain later when identifying objects. Such problems may well be suited to solution on a pipeline consisting of an instruction pipeline architecture feeding into a message-passing architecture. However, to determine if such a pipeline of heterogenous architectures was to work effectively, it would be necessary to determine how many tasks there are to pass through the pipeline, the relative processing speeds of the two different *processors* and the cost of priming the pipe. Against this must be considered the possibility of using the message-passing architecture in such a way as to carry out the work of the instruction pipeline (or the instruction pipeline to be elongated to carry out the coarser grain parallelism).

Many problems can be seen to fit this model and even if this does not lead to dedicated architectures being realized the approach will offer a useful juncture in the path from specification to implementation.

SYSTOLIC ARRAYS

A systolic array can be considered to be a pipeline that has been generalized to two (or possibly more) dimensions. Data flow through each of the dimensions in only one direction, but the rate of flow through the dimensions may not be constant and may be computationally dependent. All of the pipeline models described in the previous sections can be generalized to be *systolic*. However, by their history they tend to be special-purpose components.

Kung [1982] and others have studied algorithms and architectures that are amenable to being presented in two dimensions. This was studied with a view to fabricating special-purpose VLSI chips that are known as *systolic arrays*. A systolic array is a collection of simple processing elements. These elements are linked together in a pattern dictated by the problem (possibly a square link to the four nearest neighbours, but it may be more complicated). Data enter at the perimeter of the array, and then pass from one processing element to the next one(s) (Figure 4.7). Processing elements may all perform the same operation or different operations. The name *systolic* stems from the analogy of pumping data through the array and pumping blood through the body by the heart.

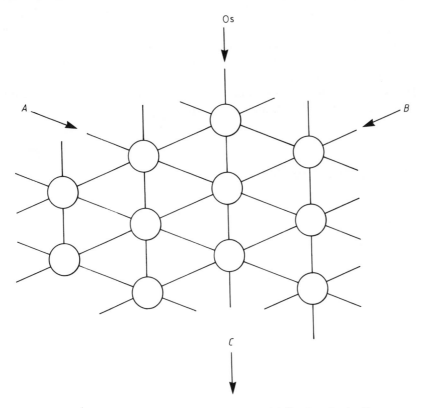

Figure 4.7 *Systolic array for the matrix multiplication* $C = A \times B$

In the example (Figure 4.7) all processing elements perform the same operation and so this particular configuration could be classified as an array processor. However, the way in which the information flows is very in keeping with the pipeline model. Each processing element receives three inputs:

- one from directly above (i.e. a sub-total)
- one from above left (i.e. an element of the array A)
- one from the above right (i.e. an element of the array B).

The processing element calculates the sum of the sub-total with the *A* element multiplied by the *B* and then passes on values to its neighbours:

- the new sub-total is passed downwards
- the value received from above right is passed below left
- the value received from above left is passed below right.

Initially values of rows of *A* are fed in at the upper left side (one row each cycle); similarly rows of *B* are fed in on the upper right side. An empty matrix (i.e. of zeros) is fed in from above. Careful design of the system assures that values of *A*, *B* and *C* arrive simultaneously at a processing element and the appropriate calculation is carried out. Processing elements not receiving: all three are acting as messengers and should pass on the values in the correct direction. Eventually values of rows of *C* will appear at the bottom of the systolic array and to the sides will be values rows of *A* and *B* respectively, which can be discarded.

The specialist purpose of systolic arrays means that they are often treated as specialist units rather than whole computers.

4.8 CHAPTER REVIEW

- A pipeline consists of a number of processors executing different instructions
- Information flows along the pipeline in one direction
- The more consecutive times a pipeline is used, the better the performance
- The overhead of using a pipeline is the pipe priming time
- A pipeline in more than one dimension is sometimes called a *systolic array*
  —The truly general case with information flowing in any direction is dealt with in Chapter 6.

5 Shared Memory Processing

A shared memory machine consists of a number of processors all having access to a single shared memory.

In the dishwashing scenario this would be the case were all the helpers had access to every item. Susie could take a knife Joe was in the midst of washing and attempt to put it away.

Protocols need to be introduced to avoid clashes over the use of variables.

A notice board can be considered as an example of a shared memory environment. All members of a department can inspect and post notices. Many protocols are employed to control the use of such boards:

- new notices are stuck in blank spaces
- the boss can remove any notice
- any out-of-date notice can be removed
- notices on the board cannot be amended
  etc.

Sometimes notice boards (especially electronic ones) are moderated: all notices are sent to a moderator who determines if they should be displayed and for how long.

A common variant on the shared memory architecture is to allow each processor a private (or cache) memory in which to keep private copies of variables currently in use.

> The dishwashers could be provided with a table on which they place items they are currently *not processing*. Anyone can take or put items on the table. This would prevent Susie from snatching the knife; it would not, however, stop her trying to put it away before it was clean or arguing with Joe as to who should have it.

In this model it is assumed that the processors operate independently on their own data streams. In Flynn's terms this is MIMD, although it is somewhat difficult to see the common memory as different data streams.

There is much in common with shared memory multi-processor and systems programming. Indeed until recently the term *concurrent programming* was only associated with operating systems and real-time systems [Ben-Ari 1982].

> The words *concurrent* and *parallel* are used by different people to mean different things. There are no clear definitions. One author may call a text *concurrent processing* while another may call an identical text *parallel processing*. Of late I have avoided the word *concurrent*. I don't think I use it in this book, because on balance I think *concurrent* refers mainly to systems programming while *parallel* is more general.

In the early 1970s a shared memory machine was built at Loughborough University of Technology [Evans 1982]. Since then a number of other machines have been built and marketed, including the Alliant and Encore. Indeed this model of parallelism is very suited to the design of *own* architectures (e.g. a one-off designed, used and built by one team) and can be (relatively) easily constructed from available processors and memory. A group of workstations connected by a network to a common memory can be considered to be a shared memory processor with each processor having a private memory.

5.1 PARALLEL LANGUAGE CONSTRUCTS

A number of different constructs have been proposed that allow users to explicitly indicate where parts of their programs can be executed on separate shared memory processors. The two most widely used ones are:

● FORK and JOIN
● Cobegin

There are many variations on these constructs and the names used to describe them; some of these are presented in the following sub-sections.

1.1. FORK and JOIN

Anderson [1965] suggested statements that could be added to Algol 60 to allow for parallel processing. These include FORK, which initiates parallel tasks, and JOIN, which waits for parallel tasks to finish. Since then a number of variants on FORK and JOIN have been suggested including their use in the UNIX[1] operating system. Here the general concept of FORK and JOIN as used in parallel processing is presented.

A FORK statement can be viewed in two ways:

1. Initiating one or more new processes and continuing with the process that executed the FORK.
2. Initiating two or more new processes, the process that executed the FORK having terminated.

The first model suggests in some way that the process that executes the FORK is in some way superior to the one forked to. The second alternative makes both processes equal.

A JOIN statement can be similarly viewed in two ways:

1. Terminating one or more processes and continuing with the process that originally forked to them.
2. Terminating two or more processes and continuing with a new process. In this case the JOIN can be seen as the last statement of the terminating processes or the first statement of the new process. With joining of several processes it is important that all processes are listed to avoid the embarrassment of leaving one behind!

There are a number of ways in which FORKs and JOINs can be linked:

1. Every FORK must be matched by a JOIN.
2. Processes that are joined must come from the same FORK, but they do not need to be joined at the same JOIN operation (for example, there may be two places where processes from one FORK may be joined).

---

[1]UNIX is a trademark of Bell Laboratories.

3. Any processes that exist can be joined.

4. Forked processes need not be joined.

In its simplest form a FORK statement can be seen as similar to a procedure call, a FORK allowing another routine (process) to commence. However, unlike a sequential procedure call, with a FORK the calling process continues its execution. The calling process will at some later point contain a JOIN. At this point it will wait until the called routine has terminated, which because of parallel processing may have already happened.

```
PROCESS A              PROCESS B
:                      :
:                      :
FORK B                 :
:                      END
JOIN B
:
:
END
```

In the above example a single process A is executed until the FORK statement is reached, then process B can be initiated on a second processor, while A continues to be executed on the first processor. If process A reaches the JOIN

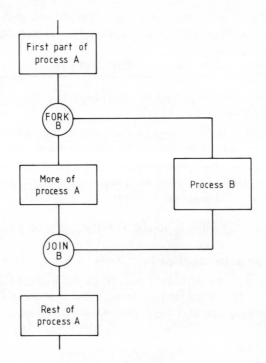

Figure 5.1 FORK and JOIN

before process B has terminated, it will suspend until B is completed. A having reached the JOIN and B having terminated the original process, A can continue (Figure 5.1).

The syntactical variations on FORK and JOIN are as numerous as proposals for their use. However, the essence of their use is that a number of processes are created by the FORK and processes are synchronized by the JOIN. A possible syntax is illustrated below:

```
task1
:
:
FORK task2, task3
:
:
GOTO task4
{end of task1}

task2
:
:
GOTO task4
{end of task2}

task3
:
:
GOTO task4
{end of task3}

task4
JOIN task1, task2, task3
:
:
```

The syntax above allows the forking by *task1* to two new tasks (2 and 3) which will execute in parallel with each other and the remainder of *task1*. When all three tasks have terminated, task 4 will be allowed to commence.

This gives rise to the question 'What if the first statement of *task4* wasn't a JOIN, but an executable statement. Could task 4 be started before the others have terminated?' This issue is partially discussed below.

1.2 Process Declaration

A variation on the FORK and JOIN model is based on *process declarations*. Processes when created can be considered to exist in a state of *suspended animation*. They may be put in that state at the start of the program or they may be created by statements in other processes. Such processes thus can be animated via a call such as a FORK. A process may only be animated once or may be instantiated a number of times. In Concurrent Pascal this explicit animation can only be used during program initialization resulting in a fixed number of processes, whereas in ADA TASKs (processes) can be created at any time during execution so there are a variable number of processes.

This model then becomes very similar to the message-passing model discussed in Chapter 6. A complete generalization of the concept gives rise to notations such as Linda (see Chapter 8).

To avoid the blurring of issues here it will always be assumed that JOIN returns to an existent process and so in the above example this is achieved by concatenating tasks 1 and 4.

```
task1
    :

    :
FORK task2, task3
    :

    :
JOIN task2, task3
    :

    :
```

5.1.3 Cobegin

The Cobegin or parallel clause (par), as it is referred to in Algol 68, allows a structured way of denoting parallel (concurrent) execution of a set of statements. The Cobegin terminates only when all the constituent tasks have terminated (whereas JOINs need not match FORKs). The single-entry and single-exit control structure allows specification of most concurrent computations whilst maintaining ease of readability.

The general form used by Algol 68 for parallel clauses is:

```
par begin
      statement 1,
      statement 2,
        :
        :
      statement n
end
```

This allows for the all *n* statements to be executed in any order, including simultaneously. All *n* statements must terminate before the program can continue after the **end** of the parallel clause.

A syntactically correct program may contain an assignment to a variable x in both statement 1 and 2; the results of such an assignment is non-deterministic. The user has to provide the protection needed to ensure the integrity of variables such as x.

Structured languages (such as Algol 68) are better served with a structured parallel operator (of the Cobegin variety) rather than the loosely structured FORK and JOIN. Structured languages are also more able to support the use of variables local to a process, which will be amenable to programming shared memory architectures that have additionally cache or private memory available.

Cobegins are also easily nested. FORK and JOINs can also be nested but not so readily.

.2 SYNCHRONIZATION IN A SHARED 1EMORY ENVIRONMENT

Within a shared memory environment, when two processes both access the same variable care must be taken to ensure the integrity of the variable. For instance, if two processes both use a variable consider what may happen:

```
cobegin
        (a: = 100
        print (''task1'', a)),
        (a: = 199
        print (''task2'', a))
coend
```

This may result in:

```
task 1 100
task 2 199
```

or

```
task 1 199
task 2 199
```

or

```
task 1 100
task 2 100
```

or

```
task 2 199
task 1 100
```

or

```
task 2 199
task 1 199
```

or

```
task 2 100
task 1 100
```

That is assuming that the assignment to a variable and a print are indivisible operations, otherwise it is possible to imagine the two prints producing something like:

```
ttasask k 21 7654
```

the assignments of the individual bits of the numbers having truly screwed up—even altering the binary representation of the numbers!—which (generally) is not what the programmer would have wanted. An *indivisible operation* is one that once started can not be interrupted. Assignment statements are often considered to be indivisible. Usually indivisibility reflects the underlying hardware, where a single cycle is required to perform an instruction.

Sections of code that need to be protected from other processes are called *critical sections* and access to these parts must be in a controlled manner. The general approach is by *mutual exclusion* where a section of code is treated as an indivisible operation. This can prevent unintended results that may occur if two processes were to access the same pieces of data. A sequence of statements that should be treated as an indivisible operation is called a *critical section*. Two critical sections (on different processes) that are not to be executed together are said to be mutually exclusive. A number of mechanisms have been proposed for achieving such mutual exclusion in a shared memory parallel processing environment. The next sections outline some of these approaches.

5.2.1 Semaphores

Semaphores are a frequently used synchronisation mechanism. Semaphores are based on the P and V operations defined by Dijkstra [1968].

Essentially a semaphore is an integer variable which can take only non-negative values. For a given semaphore the two operations that are defined can decrement and increment the value of the semaphore. For a given semaphore s the two operations P and V are defined as follows:

P(s) delays until $s > 0$ and then decrements s by 1. The test and subtraction must be treated as an indivisible operation.

V(s) increments s by 1. This must also be an indivisible operation.

A slightly different view of the two can be represented by using the English version of the names:

wait(*s*):
when $s > 0$, *s* is decremented by 1, otherwise the process calling the wait is suspended.
signal(*s*):
if some process has been suspended on this signal, wake it up, otherwise increment *s* by 1.

Both these interpretations will lead to mutual exclusion: the difference is whether the suspended process needs to continually check if it can restart, or the current process needs to look for something to revive, as it finishes.

The following piece of code will provide a solution to the mutual exclusion problem using wait and signal.

```
integer s: = 1
cobegin
        process p1
        begin
            repeat
                wait(s)
                critical part1
                signal(s)
                rest1
            forever
        end,

        process p2
        begin
            repeat
                wait(s)
                critical part2
                signal(s)
                rest2
            forever
        end
coend
```

It can be shown that the solution above is *safe*, *live* (*free from lockout*) and *deadlock free*, assuming that neither process terminates in its critical section.

Where a *safe* solution is that the mutual exclusion is absolute, there is no possible execution that would lead to both critical sections been executed together.

A *live* solution is one where if an action is supposed to happen it will eventually do so. Note that the first definition of P and V (given above) could lead to one process being locked out. If for instance process 1 first entered its critical section and process 2 also wished to enter its critical section, then process 2 would suspend. Process 2 would every so often check if the semaphore was greater than zero. Suppose process 1 set the semaphore back to one, and quickly did the rest of its code and then wished to enter its critical section again. It is conceivable that this would all happen while process 2 was *sleeping*, and so process 2 may always *miss its go*. By ensuring the sleeping process is woken in the second definition, such a *lockout* cannot occur.

Deadlock is not possible with either definition, as always one or both processes are able to execute. Processes are said to deadlock if no process is capable of doing any useful work.

The solution above can be generalized to *N* processes, where all processes take a similar form:

```
process pi
begin
     repeat
             wait(s)
             critical part i
             signal(s)
             rest i
     forever
end
```

and all the processes can be executed together:

```
cobegin
        process p1,
        process p2,
        :
        :
        process pN
coend
```

This solution is still safe and free from deadlock; however, it is possible that one or more processes may become locked out. Ben Ari [1982] suggests a number of ways in which this problem can be overcome and *fairness* introduced while solving the mutual exclusion problem.

5.2.2 Monitors

A monitor can be viewed as somewhat like a 'Nanny' whose permission or help must be sought before any communication between two processes. Semaphores are low-level synchronization primitives; as such they are difficult to use and subject to errors on the part of the user. Monitors provide a higher-level synchronization, and are used in a structured manner and (hopefully) are less subject to errors. A monolithic monitor that took care of many *charges* would be probably equally error prone and so should be avoided.

A monitor can be described as an *abstract data type* that consists of a set of permanent variables, a set of procedures and a *body* (i.e. a sequence of statements). The body is executed when the program is initiated and provides initial values for the monitor variables. Thereafter the monitor is only accessed via its procedures. The underlying system schedules the execution of the monitor's procedures. Access to these procedures is granted to only selected processes.

A monitor can be considered to come with two guarantees:

1. The initialisation code will be executed before any contention can occur.
2. Only one of the procedures will be executed at one time.

These guarantees can be respected by ensuring that the bodies of all monitors are executed when the program containing them is started and providing mutual exclusion on the entry and exit from monitors. Additionally monitors usually are *fair*. When a calling process is blocked it is entered onto a queue (first in first out). Processes are woken in the order they are entered in the queue.

In the *kitchen sink* drama Nanny may operate a scullery as a monitor. The scullery is a room with a door and a number of cupboards. The scullery is the only place where dishes can pass from one processor to another. Nanny says 'When the scullery door is shut no one may enter.' If the door is open one person may enter, closing the door behind them to prevent anyone else entering. The person can then perform the monitored operation (e.g. deposit clean wet item on the draining board), indicate what it has done and leave the scullery, leaving the door open.

Sometimes a person (say Joe) will be unable to perform the monitored operation (e.g. the draining board may be full), in which case Nanny will tell him to enter an appropriate cupboard. As he enters the cupboard Nanny will open the scullery door.

He will remain in the cupboard until someone else (say Tom) has entered the scullery and indicates that the waited-for operation (e.g. removing something from the draining board) has been performed. Nanny then allows Tom to slip out of the room (taking care to let no one else in). She then whispers to Joe that he can come out of his hiding place, thus passing control to Joe, who has now emerged from the cupboard.

Cupboards can hold many people (!) and those in a cupboard always let the person who has waited the longest out first.

5.3 CONCURRENT PASCAL

A number of languages have incorporated the monitor concept to protect the use of global variables (e.g. Concurrent Pascal, Pascal plus, Concurrent

Euclid) [Perrott 1987]. In all these cases the bases of the monitor is built on a module structure similar to the one described earlier (Chapter 2) for the programming language Modula-2. A Concurrent Pascal program has essentially two types of components:

- Processes
- Monitors

The type Class is not considered here.

A process consists of local variables and operations on them (i.e. program statements). Monitors provide the means for communication between processes. The structure of Concurrent Pascal is very similar to that of Pascal—monitors resemble procedure definitions.

```
var DrainingBoard:monitor;
        var entry Count: 0..max;
        procedure entry Increment;
        begin
              Count: = Count + 1;
        end;
        procedure entry Decrement;
        begin
              Count: = Count - 1;
        end;
    begin
        Count: = 0;
    end;
```

This simple solution ignores the problem of full and empty draining boards.

Unlike some monitor-based languages it is necessary to explicitly initiate monitors in Modula-2 so that the variable *Count* is set to zero. This initialization statement takes the form:

init DrainingBoard

The procedures of the monitor are called by specifying the monitor name and the procedure name (plus any parameters that may be required). For example:

DrainingBoard.Increment

will be a call to the Increment procedure in the monitor DrainingBoard.

Synchronization is provided via a variable type *queue*. Queue variables must be global to all the monitor's procedures and three operators are defined that can operate on such variables:

delay
continue
empty

A delay operation on a non-empty queue is undefined. The user must provide arrays of queues and associated scheduling routines.

The example can be refined to allow for both full and empty draining boards.

```
var DrainingBoard:monitor;
      var entry Count:0..max;
            DishesReady:queue;
            BoardSpaces:queue;
      procedure entry Increment;
      begin
            if Count = max then delay (BoardSpaces);
            Count: = Count + 1;
            continue (DishesReady);
      end;
      procedure entry Decrement;
      begin
            if Count = 0 then delay (DishesReady);
            Count: = Count - 1;
            continue (BoardSpaces);
      end;
   begin
      Count: = 0;
   end;
```

A continue operation on an empty queue has null effect.

.4 *PORTABLE PARALLEL PROGRAMS*

Research workers at Argonne National Laboratory [Boyle et al 1987] have developed a set of tools that allow programs to run on almost any shared memory machines. The motivation for this work was to enable the authors to explore issues of performance and portability on a range of parallel machines.

Two languages were considered as a suitable base for this project: C and Fortran. C was chosen as the less limited of the two. Parallelism is represented at the language level by *monitors*. The implementation of monitors is achieved by a set of macros that allow portability, by hiding the machine dependencies. The basic macros needed are for:

- creating new processes
- declaring monitor variables
- initializing monitors
- entering and exiting monitors
- delaying/continuing processes in a queue.

A number of programs have been successfully implemented and run using this approach and the macros could readily be translated into other procedural languages (e.g. Pascal).

5.5 *PARALLEL RANDOM ACCESS MACHINES*

There are a number of commercially available shared memory machines [Almasi and Gottlieb 1989]. Many other models exist in prototype or on paper. There are subtle differences between various instantiations of these models which reflect some known problems in sequential models.

The RAM (random access memory) model of sequential computer memory can be generalized to represent possible shared memory architectures. This generalization is known as the PRAM (parallel random access memory) model where n processes can make synchronous simultaneous access to a common memory [Preparata 1987].

There are a number of variants on this model and a variety of ways to resolve conflicts, one approach is to use Common PRAM while another is to use Priority PRAM:

● Common PRAM requires that all processors that can simultaneously write to a memory location, must require to write the same value. The emphasis is placed on the provision of software to ensure that different values are not attempted to be written

● Priority PRAM associates an index with processors and when simultaneous writes are required the value written will be the one associated with the processor with the lowest index. In this case the hardware must resolve any conflicts

Thus Common PRAM would not allow two processors to attempt to carry out, simultaneously, the following assignments:

x: = 3   x: = 4

whereas Priority PRAM would allow x to be assigned the value 3, assuming the first processor had the lower index.

Other schemes allow different resolution of such conflicts and the additional conflicts associated with attempts to simultaneously read and write to a single locations. These include:

● Concurrent Read Exclusive Write (CREW) PRAM
● Exclusive Read Exclusive Write (EREW) PRAM
● Arbitrary PRAM
● Collision PRAM

Essentially PRAM allows a relatively low-level resolution of the problems already described at a higher level.

Machines can also be modelled that offer some memory locations as local to particular processors while the remainder of the memory is shared between all processors. Local memory is like the concept of cache [Almasi and Gottlieb 1989]. In a sequential environment a cache offers faster access in some way more *close* to the processing unit for information currently being used. Local memory also offers this to the parallel processor, but it also offers protection from access by the other processors. Software synchronization techniques described earlier will also afford such protection, but local memory will save on some of the overheads.

6 *CHAPTER REVIEW*

- A shared memory model consists of a number of processors all having access to a single memory
- Shared memory processes are usually controlled by FORK and JOINs or Cobegin statements
- Techniques for synchronization must be used to protect the integrity of information shared between processes, mechanisms used include:
    — semaphores
    — monitors
- Variants on the shared memory machines are sometimes classified as PRAM (parallel random access machines).

6 *Message Passing*

With a message-passing programming model data are passed explicitly between processes. This can be viewed as extending *semaphores* (see previous chapter) to convey data as well as enabling synchronization. Alternatively it can be seen as the ultimate of shared memory processing where processors only have private memory.

> In the *kitchen sink* drama the person washing the dish must hand it to the person who is to dry it. Thus the synchronization comes from the fact that both people must be ready for the exchange and then the dishes (the data) can pass between them.
> Sometimes a draining board (buffer) is used to avoid the need for the provider to wait for the receiver.

1 CHANNELS

In a message-passing environment processes are linked by channels of communication. These channels allow messages to be sent by one process and received by another:

e.g. **send** expression **to** destination
     receive variable **from** source

Additionally, there may be information about the subject of the message so the two parties can agree as to what is being communicated. This may take the form of matching the type of the communication. A simple case may be when the first process sends an integer and so the second must be prepared to accept an integer.

> **send** plate **to** Tom **re** washing up
> **receive** plate **from** Dad **re** washing up

6.1.1 Naming Channels

A number of schemes have been proposed for using channels including:

- direct naming
- global mailbox
- channel naming

6.1.1.1 Direct Naming

This is perhaps the simplest scheme where the process that is to receive the message is specifically named.

e.g. **send** expr **to** process 2
  receive var **from** process 1

would send a message that can only be received by process 2 and receive a message that is sent by process 1.

This scheme works well if the two processes involved only communicate at one point. If there are a number of communications it will be difficult to match up **send**s and **receive**s. Consider the following fragments of (domestic) processes;

Process 1
  :
  if condition1 then send tea to process 2
  :
  if condition2 then send cheese to process 2
  :
Process 2
  :
  if condition3 then receive sustenance from process 1
  :
  if condition4 then receive food from process 1
  :

After their execution will:

1. sustenance be tea and food be cheese
2. sustenance be undefined and food be tea
3. sustenance be undefined and food be cheese
4. sustenance and food be undefined
5. sustenance be cheese and food be undefined

or will process 2 not complete because it is waiting for values to be input, or will process 1 not complete because it is waiting for output expressions to be accepted?

1.1.2   *Global Mailboxes*

A mailbox can be the destination of any **send** and the source of any **receive** that names that mailbox.

e.g. **send** expr **to** mailbox 1
     receive var **from** mailbox 1

The advantage of global mailboxes is also the disadvantage; that is, the sender does not have control over who will receive the message (how great an asset or loss will depend on how tedious it is considered having to trace messages). This situation is very like shared memory and again shows how *fuzzy* the borders are between the classes.

Mailboxes can be globally available but more usually are shared between a small number of processes. For example, a process cryptograph may accept input from any one of a number of processes and pass the (encoded) message on without any need for a response.

```
Process cryptograph
      do forever
            receive message from mailbox 1
            new_message = encoded (message)
            send new_message to mailbox 2

Process hello
      :
      send ''hello'' to mailbox 1
      :

Process greeting
      :
      send ''greeting'' to mailbox 1
      :
:
:
```

Several different cryptographic processes may take messages from the mailbox 1 and encode them in their special way and then pass them on.

6.1.1.3   *Channel Naming*

Channel naming can be either static or dynamic. In both cases a channel is defined to link two processes in one direction (i.e. one is the sender and the other the receiver). Two processes may be able to communicate down several channels. With static channel naming, links are set at compile time, whereas with dynamic channel naming the channels can be created and destroyed as required at run time.

e.g. **send** expr **via** channel 2
     receive var **via** channel 1

This scheme will allow the (silly) processes outlined under direct naming to become more deterministic:

Process 1

    :

    if condition1 then send tea via channel 1

    :

    if condition2 then send cheese via channel 2

    :

Process 2

    :

    if condition3 then receive sustenance from channel 1

    :

    if condition4 then receive food from channel 2

    :

The same action as described for the direct naming example can be achieved (if that is what is really required) by using a single channel.

Message passing implies the co-operation of both parties, but there are a number of possible patterns:

1. One to one
both parties are specified, by using

- their names, or
- defining a distinct channel between them, or
- defining them as the only parties who can use this mailbox

When two processes pass messages at several points (Figure 6.1), matching on a particular communication cannot be achieved by process naming; whereas it can be achieved by channel naming or mailboxes, because a dedicated channel or mailbox can be defined that links on only this one transaction.

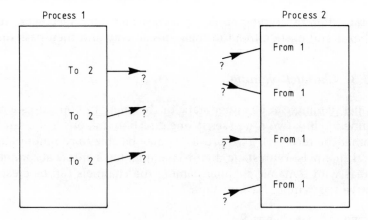

Figure 6.1 Matching communications?

> This is the simple case where Dad passes Joe a dish, which Joe is willing to accept.

2. *Many to one*

a single process is prepared to accept messages from any of a set of processes. Thus there are still only two parties to a transaction, but the sender can be one of many.

> In the *kitchen sink* drama this could be a case where there are a number of helpers capable of fetching dishes from the table, but the washer-up will only accept one dish at a time.

3. *One to many*

in this case there are many potential receivers and only one sender, there are in fact two sub-cases:

- one of the receivers will accept the communication from the sender
- all of the receivers will accept the communication from the sender

> This can be described in the *kitchen sink* drama as:
> (i) a situation where there are a number of dryers and any one of them can pick up a dish the washer-up puts on the draining board.
> (ii) Dad telling all the children to be quiet!

4. *Many to many*

in this case there are many potential receivers and many potential senders; this can also be divided into three sub-cases:

- one of the receivers will accept the communication from one of the senders
- all of the receivers will accept the communication from any one of the senders
- some combination of receivers and senders will agree on a communication

It must be pointed out that such a strategy is extremely difficult to implement. With multiple clients and multiple servers, this will in fact provide a model similar to **shared memory processing**.

> In the *kitchen sink* drama this can be illustrated by considering a larger household with several sinks each manned by a washer-up, all of whom can take dishes from any helper. Many helpers are available who take dishes from the dining table to the kitchen. Thus a dish can be delivered by any one of the helpers and processed by any one of the washer-ups.
>
> An example more in line with the third sub-case above might be if several helpers arrived bearing glasses and a single washer-up may accept them all.
>
> If a helper arrived bearing the dining table (!) several washer-ups may have to accept it for effective washing.

Which of these communication patterns can be used depends on the ways in which processes are distributed throughout the system and the manner in which they can be identified in the **send** and **receive** statements.

6.2   ASYNCHRONOUS MESSAGE PASSING

Whiddett [1987] remarks that: 'there have been few serious attempts to integrate the concept of asynchronous message passing into the framework of a high level language', and then goes on to describe the University of Rochester developed language PLITS (Programming Language In The Sky).

The concept behind asynchronous message passing is simple. The sender initiates the message and then continues with its processing. The message is accepted by the underlying system and some time later (hopefully) is delivered to its destination. A process awaiting a message will be delayed until the message arrives. This is similar to the way in which many people use electronic mail systems.

> Paul sends mail to Dave; once the underlying system has accepted the message Paul continues with whatever he has to do.
>
> Dave is probably busy doing whatever he does and is only aware of the incoming message when his mail flag is set. He will then (sometime) choose to study his mail. If Paul required a response Dave will (hopefully) issue it. If Paul needed that response he may have been sat twiddling his thumbs muttering 'Has Dave answered yet?'

Messages may not be received in the order that they are sent. Given the ability to prioritize important messages this may be seen as an asset in emergency situations. However, there are a number of disadvantages, including:

- The need for large buffers for storing unreceived messages
- The sender does not know if the message was received

The receiver can explicitly acknowledge the receipt of a message, but then should the original sender be expected to acknowledge the acknowledgement? If so, there is a danger that a system would rapidly become flooded with acknowledgements of acknowledgements of acknowledgements!

.3 SYNCHRONOUS MESSAGE PASSING

Synchronous message passing requires both the sender and receiver of a message to be delayed until its correspondent is ready. Once the message has been exchanged both processes can continue. Thus there is no real need for buffering and the state of the corresponding process is more readily available.

> With the synchronous model Tom will know that Susie has received the dish, and that they are not just piling up because she has decided to go off to the park! Of course there is always the possibility that will she disappear after accepting the dish, but Tom will become aware of this next time he tries to pass her a dish as she won't respond.

Asynchronous behaviour can be imitated in such a system by the introduction of buffer processes that will accept messages from a source and pass them on to a destination. This will make the finite size of buffers more obvious.

.3.1 Communicating Sequential Processes

Hoare [1978, 1985] proposed the use of communicating sequential processes (CSPs) as a mechanism for representing synchronous message passing and selective communication. CSPs form the basis of many languages. Perhaps the most well known is the INMOS language occam designed for programming the transputer. Occam allows a very simple form of message passing via a named channel connecting two specified processes. The specification language LOTOS is also based on CSPs but allows the sharing of a gate by many processes and messages pass between any two willing parties.

Hoare introduces the concept of an event as an instantaneous action, whose occurrence may require the simultaneous participation of other processes. Essentially what is of interest here is when two or more processes execute in parallel. Hoare represents this as:

P‖Q

That is, P occurs in parallel with Q, as opposed to:

P|Q or P‖Q

where the former means that either P or Q is executed depending on the values of associated guards and the latter means that the operations of P and Q are interleaved. These operations are particularly important in a sequential environment and are discussed in Chapter 2.

A communication is described to be an event represented by a pair:

c.v where *c* is the **name** of the channel on which the communication takes place and *v* is the value of the message.

N.B. communication within CSP is via named channels. Initial versions of CSP used the convention of naming processes; there has not been a suggestion that global mailboxes be used as this would probably lead to asynchronous communication.

An output expression from a process takes the form:

channel1 ! expression

This says: on channel1 output the value calculated by expression.

An input expression to a process takes the form:

channel2 ? variable

This says: from channel2 read the value to be stored in variable.

In the *kitchen sink* drama two processes may include the following statements:

Process washer-up

:

draining board ! clean dish

:

Process dryer

:

draining board ? wet dish

:

where draining board is the channel linking the two processes; there is a requirement that dishes are not left unattended on the draining board, they must effectively pass from hand to hand.

Channels are one-way and if two processes wish to communicate in both directions they will require two channels (i.e. one in each direction).

If the dryer wished to pass not quite clean dishes back to the washer-up, a second channel *reject* would be needed.

.4 OCCAM

Occam [INMOS 1988] is a programming language developed by INMOS for use with their transputers. A transputer is a single-chip processor with local memory and four dedicated input/output links. A transputer is either a 16- or 32-bit processor providing 10 million instructions per second, along with 2 or more Kbytes of memory. The links enable any number of transputers to be joined together to form a network of processors that can operate in parallel, although the current limitation of four links per transputer does have some bearing on the configurations possible. An occam program can be mapped onto any number of transputers, which can run in parallel and communicate by exchanging messages. The number of transputers in the network can be increased or decreased (down to a single transputer) and the occam program can still be executed without changing its description. When a program is run on a single processor there is no real parallelism. The processor is time-sharing between the different processes, in the same way that many conventional computers time-share to support many users.

Occam is based on three simple operations:

1. Assignment
2. Input
3. Output

More complex operations are formed by the use of three constructors:

1. SEQ
2. PAR
3. ALT

Additionally there are conditional and repetitive constructs.
Assignment statements take the form:

variable: = expression

Input and output to channels are represented in the same manner as in CSP, thus an input operation is expressed as:

channel2 ? variable

This will take the value on channel2 and associate it with variable. The output operation takes the form:

channel1 ! expression

This will calculate the value of expression and send the result out on channel2.

The SEQ statement dictates that the statements following must be executed one after the other, the first one terminating before the second one can commence. The ALT statement tests the guards of all the statements following and then chooses to execute a statement with a true guard. If more than one statement has a true guard the choice is non-deterministic. The PAR statement means that all the statements following can be executed together; there is no compulsion that they must be executed together. Thus the following notions in CSP and occam:

1. Sequential

```
P ; Q      SEQ
             P
             Q
```

2. Alternate

```
P | Q      ALT
             P
             Q
```

3. Parallel

```
P ‖ Q      PAR
             P
             Q
```

Indentation is important in occam. Whereas many languages are free format, indentation in occam represents components. Thus:

```
SEQ
  P
  PAR
    Q
    R
    S
```

means that Q, R and S can be executed in parallel after P has completed; whereas:

```
SEQ
   P
   PAR
      Q
      R
   S
```

means Q and R can be executed in parallel after P has completed. Additionally, Q and R must be completed before S is executed.

The sum of the square of two numbers can be represented by the following sections of pseudo-occam program:

```
CHAN OF INT intosq1,intosq2,outtoadd1,outtoadd2,result:
PAR
   VAR x:
   SEQ
      intosq1?x
      outtoadd1!x*x
   VAR y:
   SEQ
      intosq2?y
      outtoadd2!y*y
   VAR r,s:
   SEQ
      PAR
         outtoadd1?r
         outtoadd2?s
      result!r+s
```

Diagrammatically this can be represented as Figure 6.2. Where squarer1 and squarer2 both square their inputs and adder adds its inputs together (*what else did you expect!*)

The above actions of squarer1 and squarer2 were identical except for the different inputs. As processes can be named and given parameters this section of program can be rewritten as:

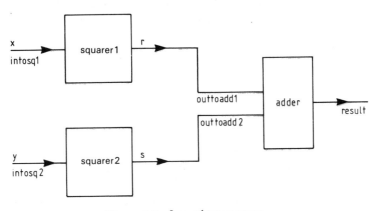

Figure 6.2 *Sum of two squares*

```
PROC square (CHAN in,out) =
   VAR x:
   SEQ
      in?x
      out!x*x
PROC sum (CHAN in1, in2, out) =
   VAR r, s:
   SEQ
      PAR
         in1?r
         in2?s
      out!r + s
CHAN OF INT intosq1, intosq2, outtoadd1, outtoadd2, result:
PAR
   square (intosq1,outtoadd1)
   square (intosq2,outtoadd2)
   sum (outtoadd1,outtoadd2,result)
```

Occam allows looping to a condition (which may be a counter) and infinite loops. For instance, if there is a stream of values to be squared:

```
PROC squarestream (CHAN in, out) =
   WHILE TRUE
      VAR x:
      SEQ
         in?x
         out!x*x
```

There are two different conditional statements in occam:

- IF
- ALT

The IF is deterministic, while the ALT is non-deterministic. In both cases the conditions are represented by guards and a process preceded by a guard that is true will be executed. The first process with a true guard in the IF list will be executed, whereas one of the processes with a true guard in the ALT list will be executed. Consider an IF statement for assigning the maximum of r and s to max:

```
IF
  r> = s
    max: = r
  r< = s
    max: = s
```

With this statement when r = s the assignment max: = r will always occur. The lazy evaluation of the IF statement allows a final guard TRUE to be used to catch those cases within an IF where none of the other guards were true.

The following is an alternative construct for assigning the maximum of r and s to max:

```
ALT
  r> =s
    max: =r
  r< =s
    max: =s
```

With this statement when r=s either the assignment max:=r or the assignment max:=s will occur.

Input statements may also be included in guards. For example:

```
WHILE TRUE
  VAR x:
  ALT
    in1?x
      out!x*x
    in2?x
      out!x*x
```

could be used when a process required input on either of its channels and would always output the input squared. If input was available on both channels a non-deterministic choice would be made between them.

Guards may be combined with boolean operators; for instance:

```
in1 ? x & r< =s
```

could be used if it was required that there be an input on channel in1 and that s was greater than r.

---

5 *LOTOS*

LOTOS [Bolognesi and Brinksma 1987] is a specification language that is applicable to distributed parallel systems. It was originally developed for the formal description of OSI (Open Systems Interconnection) architectures, but is more generally applicable.

A LOTOS specification describes a distributed parallel system via a hierarchy of process definitions (N.B. processes may consist of several sub-processes that themselves can be considered as processes). Processes are able to perform internal, unobservable actions and to interact with other processes and the outside world via events (also sometimes called interactions or actions). Events are synchronous and take place between two or more processes. An event synchronizes at a gate and may happen with or without a data exchange (here only the former is considered). Process definition is in terms of the events that can happen at its gates (the internal structure cannot be observed); see Figure 6.3.

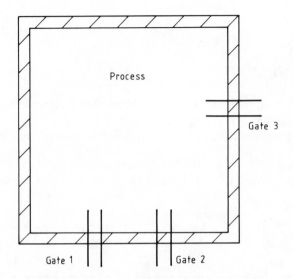

Figure 6.3   LOTOS gates

In LOTOS sequential processes are separated by a semicolon.

e.g. P1 ; P2

means that when process P1 has successfully terminated, process P2 can commence.

Parallel operations are expressed according to the gates on which the processes synchronize. The general case is when two processes P and Q communicate with each other over a set of gates:

S = [g1, ... , gn]

this is expressed as:

P|S|Q

or P|[g1, g2, g3]|Q

if the interaction is over the set of gates g1, g2 and g3.

There are two special cases:

1. Pure interleaving. When the set of synchronization gates S is empty the parallel operator |S| can be written as |||. Two processes linked by this operator can be progressed in any order. N.B. Because LOTOS is a specification language processes cannot be said to be *executed*, hence the use of *progressed*.

2. Full synchronization. When the set S consists of all gates of both processes the parallel operator |S| can be written as ||. Two processes linked by this operator must progress together except for any unobservable actions.

The alternate construct is represented as [ ] . The process that will be chosen for execution must offer an event at a gate that matches an offer from another process. Where there is more than one qualifying offer the choice is non-deterministic.

In LOTOS a value declaration takes the form:

!E

where E is a value expression describing a data value. For example, (3+5) is a value expression. The following are examples of value declarations:

! 8
! (3+5)
! max3(x, y, z).

When the name of a gate is followed by a value declaration, it is said to be a *structured event offer*.

e.g. g ! (3+5)

This indicates that the value 8 is offered at gate g.

In LOTOS a variable declaration takes the form:

? x : t

where *x* is the name of the a variable and *t* its *sort identifier* (type or domain).

e.g. ? x : integer
     ? message : text
     ? maybe : boolean.

A gate can be associated with a variable declaration.

e.g. g ? x : integer

This indicates that at gate g there is an *offer to accept* an integer value.

At a gate there may be a number of value declarations and variable declarations. Synchronization between two processes may occur at such a gate if both processes are able to offer an action that is acceptable to both, for which all attributes are matched.

The sum of the square of two numbers can be specified as:

```
Specification sumsquare [in1, in2, out]
(*Defines a three-gate process that accepts two natural numbers, in any
order, then offers the sum of their squares at the output gate. The operations
for addition and square should also be defined as part of the abstract
data type associated with this specification, but here their meaning is
assumed.
Ignores problems of termination and overflow*)
behaviour
        ((in1 ? x : nat
        ||
        in2 ? y : nat);
        g ! square x ! square y)
        |[g]|
        g ? r : nat ? s : nat ; out ! r + s
endspec (*sumsquare*)
```

The above is a specification of a solution to the problem of finding the sum of squares, not a suggested implementation.

The gate g could be hidden between the processes using it, if it was not to be used by any other processes.

```
hide g in
        (((in1 ? x : nat
        ||
        in2 ? y : nat);
        g ! square x ! square y)
        |[g]|
        g ? r : nat ? s : nat ; out ! r + s)
```

LOTOS allows a number of conditional constructs, both of the form of guarded expressions and generalized choice. Conditionals can be associated with offers at gates. For example:

```
g ? x : nat [x ≤ 3] ; g1 ! x
|[g]|
g ? y : nat [y ≥ 3] ; g2 ! y + 3
```

These will synchronize only on the value of 3. Once the interaction has taken place the obtained expression is:

```
g1 ! 3
||
g2 ! 6
```

CHAPTER REVIEW

- Message passing processes can only share data by explicitly passing them from one process to another (or more generally from a set of processes to another set),
—all other data are private
- Messages are passed along *channels* linking processes.
- Asynchronous message passing allows a message to be sent and then *hang* around until it is needed
- Synchronous message passing needs all parties to agree to a communication.

7 *Other Models*

In the preceding chapters models of parallelism have been introduced that are based on hardware models. There are many other proposed models of parallelism. Some of the proposed models are sub-sets of the models previously described, others are defined in an attempt to distance the model from the underlying realisation.

In this chapter a number of models will be examined that can be considered to be *orthogonal* to those models previously described. They add *style*, not parallelism. The power of these models is in their ability to specify problems.

The dishwashing example may be described as a transformation of dirty dishes into clean dishes.

A more formally worded specification may be sufficient to lead to a number of implementations, e.g.:

- a number of people co-operating in one of the manners described earlier,
- a dishwashing machine
- a dustbin and delivery van—the dirty stuff goes in the bin and the van delivers clean dishes!

In some cases architectures can be developed that closely match the programming model. However, these architectures can always be classified according to one (or a combination) of the models described in the previous chapters.

The dishwasher is essentially an array processor, with each dish (piece of data) having the same operation performed on it simultaneously with all the other dishes.

Some of the models have been developed for specific applications (mainly in the field of artificial intelligence). These do not vary in the underlying models from those already described but the way in which the programming model is represented may vary radically.

This can be likened to changing the *kitchen sink* drama to a Dutch family *spring cleaning their house*.

The processors are different, and so are the tasks and language but the potential for parallelism in the underlying models is similar to that in the washing-up example.

For instance, the removal of furniture may be undertaken:

- in a sequential manner by mother
- father may direct an army of brainless clones
- the family may stand in a line passing items of furniture down the line etc.

7.1 FUNCTIONAL PROGRAMMING

Many programming languages are called functional languages. Not all of the proposed languages have been implemented and this may well be due to the difference between imperative (i.e. conventional or procedural) and functional languages. The design of a functional language is not influenced by any machine, whereas imperative languages are influenced by one or a set of machines. Thus a functional program concentrates on *what* the program is to do rather than *how* it is to do it.

The role of the *specification* is particularly important in the realms of functional programming, where the specification contains details of what is expected of the program. The functional program merely adds details; ideally there should be no need for this stage but specification languages are not (yet) that far advanced.

The functional program is derived from the specification of a problem by devising the necessary equations and data structures. These will then lead to a set of definitions of the properties and computational rules. Thus the three concepts on which functional programming is based can be classified as:

1. function applications
2. expressions
3. recursive data structures

These coupled with no side-effects and the lack of inherent sequentiality provide an interesting basis for parallel processing.

The functional programming model can be further divided into the applicative model and dataflow (or single assignment) model. Applicative programming has its roots in logic and mathematics. Church's lambda calculus is sometimes referred to as the first functional programming language (he had no computer to influence the language design). LISP was the first real applicative functional programming language. LISP is a list-processing language designed by McCarthy at MIT in the late 1950s. A LISP program is composed of function calls rather than program statements and this gave rise to the name *functional programming*. Unfortunately (as far as functional programming is concerned) LISP was later adapted for specific computers and lost some of its functional properties. Many other functional languages have been designed, including Scheme, ML, Hope and Miranda; not all of these are pure functional languages, containing in some cases assignments and referencing; and not always relying on lazy evaluation.[1]

An alternative classification of functional programming languages is that of dataflow. In a dataflow programming model a copy of each result produced by a process is passed to each process wishing to consume that value. Processes are executed as soon as all the values required are available or in the case of lazy evaluation only when the value they produce is needed. There is no concept of the *sharing* of data. A number of dataflow languages have been proposed, including Lucid, ID and Val. Dataflow machines were developed at MIT [Dennis 1980; Arvind and Kathail 1981] and at Manchester [Gurd et al 1985].

1.1 Applicative Programming

Applicative programming models are based on the operations of functions. Simply a function describes the relationship between an input and an output.

> The dishwash function takes a dirty dish as its input and produces as its output a clean dish.

The implementation of the function is not part of this description.

> Any way in which the dirty dish becomes a clean dish is acceptable, including the buying of a new one. The fact that it is a different dish is unimportant.

Applicative languages consist of a set of functional forms for combining functions into new ones and an application operation for applying a function to an argument and producing a value.

A function that doubles an integer may be represented as a mapping of an integer on to an integer:

---

[1]Lazy evaluation may in fact limit potential parallelism, as can be seen later.

double:int→int

where:

fun double x = x + x

Thus when the function **double** is applied to the integer 3 the value produced is 6:

double 3
6

Functions can be applied to the results of other functions:

double (double 3)
12

or they can be applied as *curried* functions [Bird and Wadler 1988], where one function is applied to another function to reveal a new function. For instance, a *curried* function **add** can be defined as adding an integer, which can be applied to an integer to give a third integer:

fun add x = fn y = > x + y

Other functions can be defined in terms of this partial function, for instance:

succ = add 1

So:

succ 5
6

Functions can be defined in terms of other functions, for instance a function to add together a sequence of numbers may be defined in terms of a function that splits the work in two:

```
fun sum n = halfsum (1,n)
fun halfsum (low,high) =
            if (high = low) then high
            else halfsum (low,mid) + halfsum (mid + 1,high)
            where mid = (low + high) div 2
```

This definition of the summation process contains a great deal of potential parallelism; however, it must be remarked that the parallelism stems from the algorithm chosen to represent the summation problem, not the functional representation. Given a number of processors, different halfsums can be calculated on each and the results then gathered together.

A language based on lazy evaluation may prevent this parallelism being exploited, as it would always wish to complete the evaluation of:

halfsum (low,mid)

before bothering to compute:

halfsum (mid + 1,high)

in case the former failed and meant there was no need to evaluate the latter. Peyton-Jones [1989] suggests that a popular proposal for avoiding this is to allow the programmer to annotate code to indicate where there is potential parallelism; however, the choice can be left to the compiler, but it will be an easier chore if the demand of lazy evaluation is removed from some operations.

A functional parallelizing compiler will face similar problems to those discussed in Part 2. There will be more emphasis on tasks that can be run in parallel being viewed as definitely useful or speculatively useful.

The great advantage in the field of parallel processing is not that applicative programs allow parallelism to be explicitly represented, rather that such programs have the ability to allow parallel evaluation where ever data dependencies permit it.

.1.2   Dataflow

A dataflow program is driven by the need for the data to flow through the system. This is as opposed to the conventional programming model whereby control statements dictate which order statements are executed in. Thus a dataflow program statement of the form:

$(A+B) \times (C-D)$

would indicate that the values for A, B, C, and D must be computed, whereas a conventional programming model would only allow this statement to be considered correct if the values of A, B, C, and D were already available.

Dataflow systems can be based either on *lazy* or *greedy* evaluation (also known as *demand driven* and *data driven*). With lazy evaluation the statement that reveals the result of the program is identified, and then the values required to calculate that are identified; and so on back through the program until a statement that can be computed is reached and so the answer will be calculated. Greedy evaluation calculates all values as soon as possible. The disadvantage with greedy evaluation is that some values that are not actually required may be calculated. However, in this case there is no need to calculate the flow through the program before calculating any values.

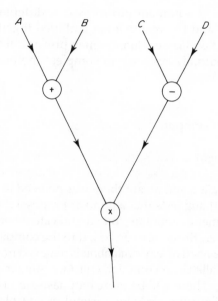

Figure 7.1 *Graphical representation of* $(A+B)\times(C-D)$

Dataflow programs are particularly amenable to graphical representation. Each operation can be represented as an *actor* and linked by directed by arcs. For instance, a graphical representation of the earlier statement is shown in Figure 7.1. Most dataflow languages are based on the single assignment rule:

> *A variable may only be assigned to once in the area of the program in which it is active.* Additionally, as with applicative languages they are free of side-effects, and any effects tend to be local [Ackerman 1982].

To overcome some of the above strait-jacket some languages introduce the concept of *histories*. For instance, a variable X used in an iteration can have associated with it a vector of values, e.g.

{1, 3, 4, 7, ...}

would show that X contained the value 1 after the first iteration and 3 after the second. All these values should be accessible. Thus the new value of X could be defined in terms of, say, the sum of its last two values.

7.1.3 Functional Architectures

Although functional languages are considered to be implementation independent, once they are used to write *parallel programs* some knowledge of the architecture is needed. This will ensure the model of parallelism of the algorithm represented by the functional program is similar to that of the architecture.

Dataflow programs are based on very-fine grained parallelism (i.e. the processes are very small). Most of the work on architectures for dataflow programs is based in research labs at MIT, Manchester and the Electronic Laboratory in Japan. An ideal dataflow machine is based on the message-passing model, with no overheads or delay on communications. The processors would only need to be small, such as those in a systolic array.

Architectures for applicative programs are much more diverse. Once again these are essentially of a research nature; prototypes exist based on the following models:

- message passing (transputers)
- shared memory
- array processors

In the UK much of the work was funded by the Alvey directorate (e.g. ALICE, Flagship and GRIP projects).

.2 *LOGIC PROGRAMMING*

Logic programming languages (such as Prolog) are sometimes described as *declarative* programming languages and classified along with functional languages. Here they are considered separately because functional programming is usually considered general purpose whereas logic programming is seen as specific to artificial intelligence. Prolog [Clocksin and Mellish 1981] is the predominant logic programming language; variations include parallel versions such as Concurrent Prolog [Shapiro 1986] and Parlog [Gregory 1987].

Logic programming languages are based on symbolic processing as opposed to the numeric processing of languages such as Fortran.

> With Prolog a program reasons from a set of facts about the family and an evaluation order: that Thomas is 8 years old, wears a red jumper and is older than his brother Joe. Whereas a Fortran program given the number of dishes to wash, the time per dish and a suitable algorithm, calculates that the rate at which clean dishes are produced is one every 37.5 seconds.

Simplistically a logic program consists of a sequence of *clauses* of the form:

$A \leftarrow B1, B2 \ldots, Bn$

If all the **B**'s are true then **A** is true.
  Three basic kind of statements can be formed from these clauses:

1. Assertion

    A

> brother (Thomas,Joe)
> *many logic programming examples come from family ties*

2. Goal statements

    ←B

> father (x,Joe)

3. Conditional

    A←B1, B2, ... ,Bn

> grandpa (x,z)←father (x,y), father (y,z).

There is a need to designate searching strategies for determining goals. One goal may only be solved by solving all sub-goals; another may be solved by solving only some sub-goals. An important process in the solving of goals is *unification*, the process of determining the most general substitutions needed to make two expressions *identical*. This gives rise to a great deal of potential parallelism, which Hogger [1984] classified as:

- **AND-parallelism**, where a number of sub-goals can be solved at once
- **OR-parallelism**, where many potential ways of solving a goal are tried at once (not all sub-goals need to be finished once a successful path is found)
- **Stream-parallelism**, where once a call has produced a part of some structured data, another call can consume that substructure

To take advantage of such parallelism requires that the semantics of the language allow it and that the style of programming does not hide the potential (which is the case with Prolog but not the parallel variations). There are claims [Hogger 1984] that a 20-fold increase in performance can be achieved when parallelism is applied to the unification process.

2.1   Architectures for Logic Programming

The base model of parallelism for logic programming is perhaps less important than the interconnection of processors. A tree-structure is the ideal as this allows easy allocation of sub-goals. Reconfigurability is also useful, as different goals will have varying numbers of sub-goals. For solving some goals array processing may be sufficient but others will require MIMD flexibility. Possible architectures include:

- A tree of message-passing processors
- An array processor (preferably reconfigurable like the Connection Machine)

Uhr [1987] suggests that a heterogeneous architecture composed of both of the above would be a better design, if there was good communication between the components.

.3   OBJECT-ORIENTED PROGRAMMING

Object-oriented programming is based on the concept of an object (as are object-oriented specifications and design). The boundary between what is an object-oriented language and what is not is very fuzzy: most certainly Eiffel [Meyer 1988] is and Fortran is not, but languages such as Simula and Modula-2 are on the boundary.

> I chose to put Simula and Modula-2 in with sequential languages because they were designed to be executed on sequential not parallel architectures, but it is feasible to envisage implementations that will execute on parallel hardware.

An *object* is a self-contained entity with its own private data and a set of operations to manipulate those data. Any access to the data of an object must be via the object's operations. Two main techniques are associated with the objects: encapsulation and inheritance.

Encapsulation of data and operations allows objects to appear opaque and so when a particular operation is required on an operand the object is prompted, by either message passing or operator overload. The object then chooses the necessary operations. Objects can be considered as an instance of a *class*. Where a class is a description of a set of objects, Meyer likens a class to a skeleton for describing a *book*, having, say, a field for the author and another for the title. An object from this class may be:

Bertrand Meyer
Object-oriented Software Construction

Most object-oriented programming languages allow the concept of *inheritance* where one object can use another without any need for redefinition. This is usually achieved by a message-passing strategy that allows the correct access mechanism to be achieved. Some object-oriented languages allow the concept of *multiple inheritance* where one object may be defined in terms of a number of other objects.

The object-oriented approach is well suited to decentralized hardware, as each encapsulation of an object can be envisaged to exist as a separate process. Objects are usually activated when they receive a message, and so a suitable parallel implementation may be based on the message-passing model. However, this is a gross oversimplification of problems that have not as yet been fully addressed [Harland 1986].

Perhaps the most useful thing that can be said of object-oriented programming is that it neither hides nor enhances parallelism and that it will be equally difficult to implement an object-oriented program on one class of parallel architecture as another.

An exception to the above statement is the Parallel Object-Oriented Language (POOL) developed at Philips Research Laboratory, Eindhoven [America 1987]. POOL is a formally based language that allows parallelism by making no distinction between processes and objects.

7.3.1 Object-oriented Architectures

Object-oriented programming is considered to be implementation independent; unfortunately this does not mean that it maps easily onto any hardware. Superficially processes and objects serve the same purposes, and so an object should be mapped onto a processor. This, however, is not the end of the story. The strength of the object-oriented approach comes from the use of classes, encapsulation and inheritance and it is the representation of these in hardware which creates the real problems.

The problems of providing effective management of objects by hardware has been studied by a number of groups [Meyrowitz 1986]. Parallel hardware for object-oriented programming is still in its infancy but is usually based on the message-passing model. Possible solutions may be offered by the Rekursiv chipset [Harland and Beloff 1986] or the two hardwares that Philips are involved in designing:

- DOOM (Decentralized Object-Oriented Machine)
- PRISMA (PaRallel Inference Storage MAchine).

4 ADDING PARALLELISM

Many of the proposed parallel programming languages have been created by taking an existing sequential programming language and introducing parallel constructs. There is a strong argument in favour of this approach. Programmers already know how to use the sequential part of the language; all they need to learn is how to handle the parallel constructs. In general this approach has not been standardized, resulting in many hybrids of the same language, in some cases designed to be executed on the same machine (there are at least three variations on C for programming transputers). Also the same constructs may have subtly different meanings in different languages (e.g. does **SIM** mean the processes *can* be done simultaneously or that they *must* be executed simultaneously?).

An alternative approach is to develop a basis of parallelism that can be added to existing languages. With this the concepts of parallelism will remain although the base language may change.

4.1 Linda

Linda [Carriero and Gelernter 1989] as such is not a language for parallel processing. It is a small number of operations that can be added to a base language to create a parallel processing dialect. To some extent the approach is no different from early attempts to add FORK and JOIN to Fortran or Algol to create parallel processing languages. However, Linda can be embedded in a variety of base languages. Linda can be considered to be orthogonal to its base: the operations of Linda although enriching the base should not alter the ways in which the base language can be used. CLinda (i.e. C with the operations of Linda added) can be used as C alone or with the Linda constructs. The main work on Linda has been to add it to C and Fortran, but work is in progress on the following bases:

- Modula-2
- C++
- PostScript
- Scheme

The concept of Linda is based on the tuple space model of parallel processing. Processes and data can be considered to be *objects* floating in tuple space. *Sender* and *receiver* processes communicate by the sender creating a *data object* that it releases into the tuple space; the receiver can examine such objects, hence the communication takes place. Processes are generated in a similar manner, only they are considered to be *live tuples* that can carry out their own process and then become *data objects*. Linda would appear to be able to be used to represent most models of parallelism (with the exception of array processing and some pipelines).

Linda provides four basic operations:

1. in
2. rd
3. out
4. eval

The first two are used for reading tuples: *in* removes the tuple read from the tuple space, *rd* leaves the tuple to be read by other processes. The others are used to create new tuples, *out* passing data objects and *eval* generating live objects.

Tuples exist independent of their creators. Tuples are matched by element type and position; creation of tuples is non-blocking. However, reading of tuples will block if there is no match, and where there are a number of matches a non-deterministic choice will be made between the matching tuples. Tuples can be grouped together to yield a variety of data structures.

7.5 CHAPTER REVIEW

- The other models can be considered orthogonal to those models described in earlier chapters
- The functional model concentrate on *what* the program is to do rather than *how* it is to be done
- Functional programming models can be divided into two parts:
  - applicative programming models based on the operations of functions,
  - dataflow models where programs are driven by the need for data to flow through the system
- Logic programming models are based on symbolic processing. Parallelism is found in four ways:
  - OR-parallelism
  - AND-parallelism
  - Stream-parallelism
  - Unification-parallelism

- The object-oriented model is based on the concept of encapsulating data and its operations together into an object
- Objects can be allocated to processors
- Linda is a small number of operations that can be added to a base language to create a parallel processing language. The model of parallelism will depend on the base.

8 Remarks

A variety of programming models have been introduced in Part 1 of this book. Emphasis has been placed on those models that mirror hardware architectures. Software engineers would argue that the progamming model should be well suited to the problem, not the hardware. However, each of the parallel hardware models presented were designed to be well suited to the solution of a particular set of problems.

The models' classifications are flabby (some might even say gross) and their boundaries are fuzzy. More specific classifications could be used. Hockney [Hockney and Jesshope 1988] has developed a set of parameters for characterizing the architectures of parallel machines. Such characterizations aim to highlight the differences between machines and it is fairly unlikely that two machines would have the same profile. Thus while such classifications are excellent for describing the power and capabilities of a certain machine, the large amount of detail prevents the generalized statements that have been made in the earlier chapters about groups of architectures.

Most problems are suitable for implementation on a variety of architectures. Determining which architecture is *best suited* to a particular problem is an issue that needs to be addressed by the software engineering community. To a large extent the approach currently taken is to:

- choose the parallel architecture that will give the best performance for the amount of money available

- implement all the problems that need parallelism on that architecture

This, however, creates problems when the target architecture changes: a change in the number of processors or the underlying programming model will probably mean going back to square one and re-solving the problem, or the development of a clever underlying 'compiler' that will 'transform' the existing program into something suitable for the new architecture.

Producing compilers for sequential programs to run on sequential architectures is a well researched area [Aho et al 1986]. There is still a great deal of work to be done before there is such a body of knowledge for parallel compilers. Most of the existing work is related to compiling Fortran programs to work on a limited number of processors [Almasi and Gottlieb 1989].

In the following chapters techniques will be introduced to help transport programs from one architecture to another; they will also provide guidelines for the compiler writer. Neither transporting programs nor writing compilers are easy tasks and the techniques presented can be considered to be *recipes* which require an excellent cook and a pinch of salt. There is no attempt to say that the transportation will be achieved easily, indeed there are even difficulties in transporting within the same model. Without this knowledge there is little hope for general methodologies for developing and maintaining parallel software.

The future may well relieve the programmer of the need to understand the underlying hardware [Chandy and Misra 1988]. However, there will still be a need for some knowledge to be had by some people of the underlying hardware.

PART 2

TRANSFORMATION TECHNIQUES

9 *Altering the Number of Processes*

In an ideal world there would be no need to consider altering the number of processes within a system, because each processor would run infinitely fast and there would be an infinite supply of processors. Programs would be written in the style the author thought most elegant. Reality is more closely associated with finite quantities. To achieve a required performance it may be necessary to group together a number of processes onto a single processor or divide a monolithic process between several processors. The target architecture may only have a limited number of processors and the overhead of *time sharing* a single processor between a number of processes may be greater than the cost of transforming the processes mapped onto it into a single process. There may be a total mis-match between the power of the processors available and the number of processes required, in which case it may be necessary to merge some processes and split others.

There is an argument that can be applied at this point which goes something like this:

The algorithm must fit the hardware architecture.

which implies that even at the highest level of problem solving there is a need for a detailed knowledge of the hardware.
Here it is assumed that algorithms are chosen without a detailed knowledge of the hardware, but as a reasonable representation of the problem in hand [Ibrahim et al 1989]. It is then possible that the solution will be mappable onto a number of architectures.

When there is a mis-match between the number of processes and the number of processors, there is a need to change the number of processes by which a problem is represented and this may be to create more or fewer processes. Two special cases of this are the mapping of a parallel program on to a single processor and the detection of parallelism in a sequential program.

> The dishwashing scenario may change if the eldest child leaves home and Mum produces identical quadruplets!

9.1   *DETECTION OF PARALLELISM WITHIN EXPRESSIONS*

Arithmetic expressions of the form:

$A+B\times C+D\times E\times F\times G+H+I$

can be represented as a tree structure (Figure 9.1). Any arithmetic operations that appear at the same level in the tree representation of the expression, may be executed in parallel on separate processors. Boolean expressions can be handled in a similar way.

> This is the way that Joe does *difficult* multiplication, if he wants 45×32:
>
> - 'Mum what's 45×2?'
> - 'Dad what's 45×30?'
> - 'Tom what's $90+1350$?'
> - '1440'

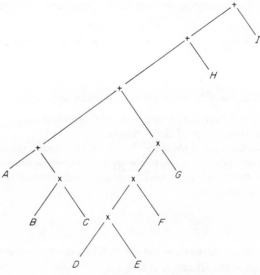

Figure 9.1   *A tree representation of $A+B\times C+D\times E\times F\times G+H+I$*

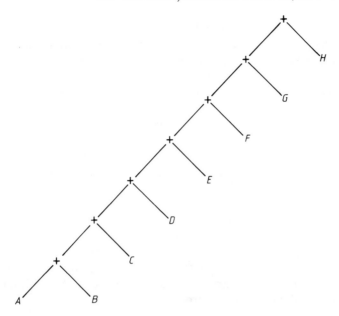

Figure 9.2 A tree representation of $A+B+C+D+E+F+G+H$

For many expressions more than one tree structure is a correct representation. Figures 9.2 and 9.3 are both correct representations of the expression:

$$A+B+C+D+E+F+G+H$$

but in the first representation there is no apparent parallelism, while there is a considerable amount in the second. The (slightly dubious) statement could be made that the first representation will take seven time units compared

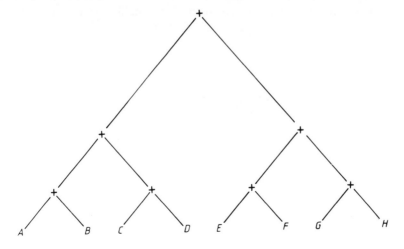

Figure 9.3 Another tree representation of $A+B+C+D+E+F+G+H$

with the three time units needed for the second. This is not strictly true since here the cost of communicating between processes is conveniently ignored.

Adapting existing parsing techniques to produce *balanced* tree representations of expressions will produce an intermediate code with more parallelism within an expression. Techniques can be developed by which a balanced binary tree is systematically costructed as an expression is parsed. A tree of single-element components is constructed by attaching the original element to the null node; the second node is *inserted above* the original component, creating a binary pair (joined by the relevant operator) with the original element the left daughter and the new element the right daughter. Additional elements are always inserted in the same manner: if the last addition was a right-hand daughter the new element must be added higher up the tree, at the first vacant slot. In some cases this will be at the top of the tree and the height will be increased by 1.

Unary minus is handled by marking the operand to be negated, as is the normal parsing practice. The process can be extended to allow for bracketed expressions and the like. Three criteria are applied to the addition of sub-trees to a partially constructed tree:

1. Any increase in the overall height of the tree caused by the insertion process should be kept to the absolute minimum. This is so the number of levels in the tree will continue to be minimized.

2. An insertion at the top of the tree is preferable to extending the tree below its lowest level. This provides for future extensions to the tree. If the tree is extended below the lowest level the next insertion will also extend the height of the tree, whereas if the tree is extended above all existing levels, the next insertion may not extend the overall height of the tree.

3. A sub-tree should be placed in the first available position in the tree, provided the previous conditions are met. This, again, is done to allow further extensions to the tree, so that the maximum number of vacant nodes is available for successive iterations.

The same concept can be used to add elements of different weights, for instance multiplication may be four times heavier (slower) than addition, and so the introduction of an element that multiplies may be treated as adding a sub-tree with four levels.

Simple assignment statements are handled by defining each statement to be a variable followed by an assignment symbol and an expression. The assignment symbol is given a higher precedence than other operators. Thus a sub-tree will be created, of level i. The value of the variable assigned to will be available at this level and any subsequent expressions that use this value must ensure that references to it are at a higher level. See Figure 9.4.

There are a number of other similar algorithms [e.g. Baer and Bovet 1968; Ward 1974; Evans and Smith 1977] in which a variety of different intermediate forms are produced and it is fairly easy to find an expression that is handled better by one method than another. Some algorithms take

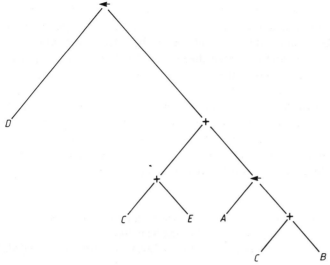

Figure 9.4 *A tree representation of:*
$$A \leftarrow B + C$$
$$D \leftarrow C + E + A$$

advantage of associative and commutative properties of expressions. It is difficult to reason whether or not such approaches are acceptable; the arguments usually revolve around possible underflow or overflow, which are far from impossible when expressions are long. Brackets are mostly treated with respect; Kuck et al [1972] have suggested the introduction of *special inviolable parentheses* to protect delicate numerical calculations.

There is a great deal more that can be considered here but it must be realized that very few programs incorporate expressions with several operands. Knuth [1971] indicates that most expressions contain one or two operators (including the assignment).

Rather like the chances of multiple births!

---

2 *PARALLELISM IN TREE STRUCTURES*

In the previous section it was shown how by examining the tree representation of an arithmetic expression it was possible to detect parallelism. Parsing is not the only place in computing where trees are used: search strategies (including those in combinatorial searches and logic programming) often use tree representations. Manipulating the shape of the tree can provide more potential parallelism in searches, as it does for arithmetic expressions.

Search problems can be represented by a tree. The root of the tree represents the original problem to be solved, and this problem is divided into a number of sub-problems that need to be solved. Sub-divisions continue (giving the tree structure) until there is no further need for division as the sub-goals' solutions are found. The final solutions are known as *terminal nodes* or *leaves* of the tree. Other nodes (representing sub-goals) are known as *non-terminal nodes*. With search trees representing the goals and sub-goals to be solved, the solution can be found by traversing the tree. In some instances it is not always necessary to solve all sub-goals to find a solution to the original problem. Thus it is not always necessary to visit all nodes of the tree structure to solve a particular problem.

If a family relationship program is to search for a brother of Susie, once one is found there is no point in continuing searching.
However, if all brothers were required the whole tree would need to be searched.

A search tree where all nodes must be visited to determine a particular goal is called an *AND*-tree whereas a tree which represents the case where not all nodes need to be visited is called an *OR*-tree. With conventional sequential implementations the tree's nodes would be visited left to right (or right to left) and down and up. Thus there is a deterministic ordering that dictates which of the sub-goals will be found in an *OR*-tree and an ordering associated with the results from an *AND*-tree. Before a parallel version is produced it will be necessary to establish if the determinate nature is important.

Simplistically each node can be allocated to a processor; the results from terminal nodes can be computed immediately and passed back to the next node above. Maximum parallelism will be achieved with a **short and fat** tree structure and an infinite supply of processors. Alternative strategies for allocating processors to nodes will depend on the power and number of processors available along with whether the tree is *AND* or *OR*.

Consider the following simple example (in pseudo-Prolog), of the relationships within a family:

```
male (Roy)
male (Tom)
male (Joe)
female (Susie)
father (Roy, Tom)
father (Roy, Joe)
father (Roy, Susie)
brother (X, Y):- father (Z, X), father (Z, Y), male (X), X ≠ Y
```

Given this information then the following question can be asked:

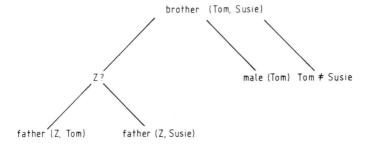

Figure 9.5 *A search tree for the goal brother (Tom, Susie)*

Is Tom the brother of Susie?

A search tree corresponding to this goal is shown in Figure 9.5.

A sequential implementation could determine the father of Tom, and then the father of Susie. Having established they were children of the same father, the sub-goal of male (Tom) would be examined and then that they were different children.

A parallel implementation could test all four terminal nodes together, i.e. establish the fathers of the children, while testing that Tom was male and was a different child to Susie. Having done that it would be necessary to check they both had the same father. An alternative parallel implementation would allow the first two terminal nodes to be established in parallel and then their results tested in parallel with the remaining terminal nodes. If the question was changed to:

Is Susie the brother of Tom?

then once the third terminal node was calculated there would be no need to solve any other sub-goals as the final goal will be false. Thus there can be an argument for working out the simplest goals first if they may negate the need for further work.

There is much more work and potential for parallelism in a larger example: consider the fact that children have two parents. Recursive relationships may make potential parallelism difficult to find.

.3 DETERMINING PARALLELISM BETWEEN BLOCKS OF ʼROGRAMS

At a coarser grain of parallelism, a single processor may be expected to execute a number of statements, as opposed to the single arithmetic operations discussed previously. The exact size of a block is difficult to determine; the target architecture will generally dictate both the block size and the optimum grain of parallelism for the problem.

An 8-year-old may be asked to calculate 32×45 while an undergraduate may be expected to calculate $\Pi \times 54.6$.

Here blocks will be considered to belong to one of six main areas:

1. Individual statements or parts of statements.
2. Groups of assignment statements.
3. Algol-type **blocks**.
4. Iterations of a loop.
5. Conditional statements.
6. Called procedures.

Thus in this context a block of code is either a single statement or a group of statements appearing adjacently in a program and intended to be executed one after the other in the order presented.

All the techniques for determining parallelism at this level are based on determining the dependencies between portions of programs. Attempts are made to achieve two goals:

1. Determining tasks that can be executed *at the same time*.
2. Localizing the data generated and used within a program.

The first goal often also attempts to match the number of processes executable with the physical number of processors. There are a number of potential dangers with this approach, not least that the *cost* of distributing the work over a number of processors may be greater than using a single or smaller number of processors.

The second goal will attempt to limit the amount of communication necessary between processors and so reduce the cost.

A number of potential relationships [Evans and Williams, 1980] can be recognized that may exist between two blocks (P_1 and P_2) of a program. For instance:

1. *Prerequisite*: process P_1 must fetch what it requires before P_2 stores its results.
2. *Conservative*: process P_1 must store its results before P_2 stores its.
3. *Commutative*: process P_1 may be executed before or after P_2, but not at the same time.
4. *Contemporary*: processes P_1 and P_2 may be executed at the same time, without any constraints.
5. *Consecutive*: process P_1 must store its results before P_2 fetches what it requires.
6. *Synchronous*: processes P_1 and P_2 must both have the same inputs (neither can store results until the other has fetched what it requires).

Relationships such as these can be used by programmers to represent the potential parallelism in the program or they can be used to detect potential parallelism in existing programs.

The relationships are couched in terms that could be used to describe a shared memory environment. However, they can be readily extended to a shared memory environment with each processor having private (or cache) memory; indeed this will be necessary to differentiate between some of these relationships. The relationships can also be extended to message-passing environments and the conditions then become the sending or receipt of messages, for example:

2. *Conservative*: process P_1 must have sent all its messages before P_2 sends any of its.

The relationships can also be used to describe the finer grain of parallelism associated with array or pipeline processing.

Within a process (or block of sequential code) there are a number of different ways in which variables (or whatever) are manipulated. For instance, four categories [Bernstein, 1966] can be defined that correspond to the way in which a memory location can be used within a sequence of instructions or block:

W The location is only fetched during the execution of P.

X The location is only stored during the execution of P.

Y The first operation involving this location is a fetch, a subsequent operation stores to it.

Z The first operation involving this location is a store, a subsequent operation fetches it.

The set of variables in each category for a process P_i are represented by W_i, X_i, Y_i and Z_i respectively.

Two combined categories can also be defined:

WY_i The set of variables not initialized within P_i (they use a value assigned elsewhere).
$$WY_i = W_i \cup Y_i$$

XYZ_i The set of variables changed within P_i (they are assigned a new value within P_i).
$$XYZ_i = X_i \cup Y_i \cup Z_i$$

For completeness a seventh category is defined:

V_i The set of all variables that are fetched without being stored after the execution of P_i. The calculation of V_i is, in general, a non-trivial matter, and it may be convenient to consider the full set of variables in many instances.

Five of the relationships outlined above can be seen to potentially exist between two blocks of program P_1 and P_2 that are defined by the programmer as executing one immediately after the other:

1. Prerequisite
2. Conservative
3. Commutative
4. Contemporary
5. Consecutive

The sixth relationship (synchronous) is impossible (except in the most trivial cases) within a sequential program.

In the following sub-sections, the relationships necessary between the sets representing the variable usage in the two processes P_1 and P_2 will be derived, so that the two processes can be upgraded, manually or automatically, to be *more parallel* than their original sequential presentation. First of all the case where the processes have private memories will be presented, then this will be compared with the shared memory case.

9.3.1 Private Memories

1. Prerequisite: process P_1 must fetch what it requires before P_2 stores its results. This implies that P_1 uses a location whose value may be changed by P_2, i.e.:

   $$WY_1 \cap XYZ_2 \neq \emptyset$$

   Process P_2 must not require information computed in P_1, because P_1 does not necessarily complete before P_2 fetches:

   $$XYZ_1 \cap WY_2 = \emptyset$$

   Locations changed by both P_1 and P_2 must not be used elsewhere without first being reset, as their values will be undefined:

   $$XYZ_1 \cap XYZ_2 \cap V_2 = \emptyset$$

   Note there is no need to include V_1 as this is the same as V_2 except for the changes made by P_2, because P_1 and P_2 were to originally be executed one after the other.

2. Conservative: process P_1 must store its results before P_2 stores its. This implies that a location changed by both processes is required later, and it must have the value assigned in P_2:

   $$XYZ_1 \cap XYZ_2 \cap V_2 \neq \emptyset$$

   The second process must not require information calculated in the first as it may not yet have been stored:

   $$XYZ_1 \cap WY_2 = \emptyset$$

3. Commutative: process P_1 may be executed before or after P_2, but not at the same time. The outputs from P_1 must not be needed by P_2:

   $$XYZ_1 \cap WY_2 = \emptyset$$

and vice versa:

$$WY_1 \cap XYZ_2 = \varnothing$$

Locations changed by both processes must not be used later without first being reset:

$$XYZ_1 \cap XYZ_2 \cap V_2 = \varnothing$$

as the value of such locations is undefined.

4. Contemporary: processes P_1 and P_2 may be executed at the same time, without any constraints. Within a private memory environment these conditions are identical to those for the commutative relationship.

5. Consecutive: process P_1 must store its results before P_2 fetches what it requires. This implies that a value stored by P_1 is used by P_2:

$$XYZ_1 \cap WY_2 \neq \varnothing$$

Thus process P_1 must complete before P_2 can start—they are inherently sequential.

3.2 Shared Memory

1. Prerequisite: process P_1 must fetch what it requires before P_2 stores its results. This implies that P_2 changes a value that P_1 needs, to achieve the necessary degree of protection, the last fetch by P_1 must be completed before the first store of P_2. The relationship degenerates essentially to the consecutive one.

2. Conservative: process P_1 must store its results before P_2 stores its. As with prerequisite, this relationship degenerates essentially to a consecutive one.

3. Commutative: process P_1 may be executed before or after P_2, but not at the same time. The outputs from P_1 must not be used by P_2:

$$XYZ_1 \cap WY_2 = \varnothing$$

and vice versa:

$$WY_1 \cap XYZ_2 = \varnothing$$

Locations changed by both processes must not be used later without first being reset:

$$XYZ_1 \cap XYZ_2 \cap V_2 = \varnothing$$

as the value of such locations is undefined.

4. Contemporary: processes P_1 and P_2 may be executed at the same time, without any constraints on the ordering of statements. Thus, there must be no fetching of any locations in P_1 that are stored in P_2:

$$(WY_1 \cup Z_1) \cap XYZ_2 = \varnothing$$

and vice versa:

$$XYZ_1 \cap (WY_2 \cup Z_2) = \emptyset$$

Any locations changed by both P_1 and P_2 must not be subseqently used without being reset:

$$XYZ_1 \cap XYZ_2 = \emptyset$$

Note these conditions are so strong there is no need to consider subsequent usage of variables; if the above is true then anything in V_2 will be safe to use.

5. Consecutive: process P_1 must store its results before P_2 fetches what it requires. This implies that a value stored in P_1 is used in P_2:

$$XYZ_1 \cap WY_2 \neq \emptyset$$

9.3.3   N Processes

It is possible to expand all the definitions of the relationships to apply to N processes that are defined to be executed in a sequential manner $[P_1, P_2, ..., P_N]$.

1. Prerequisite: process P_k must fetch what it requires before P_{k+1} stores its results, for all k such that $1 \leq k < N$.

2. Conservative: process P_k must store its results before P_{k+1} stores its, for all k such that $1 \leq k < N$.

3. Commutative: the set of processes $\{P_1, P_2, ..., P_N\}$ may be executed in any order, provided that:
   - only one process is executed at a time
   - once a process is initiated it must complete before another process can start.

4. Contemporary: all processes $[P_1, P_2, ..., P_N]$ can be executed at the same time or in any order.

5. Consecutive: process P_k must store its results before P_{k+1} fetches what it requires, for all k such that $1 \leq k < N$.

Again, for completeness a sixth relationship can be defined, which is impossible (except in the most trivial cases) within a sequential program:

6. Synchronous: all processes $[P_1, P_2, ..., P_N]$ must have the same inputs (none can store results until all the others have fetched what they require).

Table 9.1 shows the relationships necessary to establish these relationships between sequential processes.

Table 9.1 Conditions necessary for a single given relationship to exist between N processes

Relationship	Conditions	
	Private memories	**Shared memory**
Prerequisite	$(X_k \cup Y_k \cup Z_k) \cap ((W_{k+1} \cup Y_{k+1}) \cup \ldots \cup (W_N \cup Y_N)) = \emptyset^\dagger$ $(X_k \cup Y_k \cup Z_k) \cap ((X_{k+1} \cup Y_{k+1} \cup Z_{k+1}) \cup \ldots$ $\cup (X_N \cup Y_N \cup Z_N)) \cap V_N = \emptyset^\dagger$	as Consecutive
Conservative	$(X_k \cup Y_k \cup Z_k) \cap ((X_{k+1} \cup Y_{k+1}) \cup \ldots$ $\cup (X_N \cup Y_N \cup Z_N)) \cap V_N = \emptyset^\dagger$	as Consecutive
Commutative	as Contemporary	$(W_k \cup Y_k) \cap (X_l \cup Y_l \cup Z_l) = \emptyset^*$ $(X_k \cup Y_k \cup Z_k) \cap (X_{k+1} \cup Y_{k+1} \cup Z_{k+1}) \cup \ldots$ $\cup (X_N \cup Y_N \cup Z_N)) \cap V_N = \emptyset^\dagger$
Contemporary	$(W_k \cup Y_k) \cap (X_l \cup Y_l \cup Z_l) = \emptyset^*$ $(X_k \cup Y_k \cup Z_k) \cap (\ X_{k+1} \cup Y_{k+1} \cup Z_{k+1}) \cup \ldots$ $\cup (X_N \cup Y_N \cup Z_N)) \cap V_N = \emptyset^\dagger$	$(W_k \cup Y_k \cup Z_k) \cap (X_l \cup Y_l \cup Z_l) = \emptyset^*$ $(X_k \cup Y_k \cup Z_k) \cap (\ X_{k+1} \cup Y_{k+1} \cup Z_{k+1}) \cup \ldots$ $\cup (X_N \cup Y_N \cup Z_N)) \cap V_N = \emptyset^\dagger$
Consecutive	No conditions necessary as this implies $(X_k \cup Y_k \cup Z_k) \cap (W_{k+1} \cup Y_{k+1}) \neq \emptyset^\dagger$	

* for all k such that $1 \leq k \leq N$ and for all l such that $1 \leq l \leq N$ and $l \neq k$

† for all k such that $1 \leq k < N$

9.3.4 Message Passing

The relationships developed for the private-memories case will also serve for the message-passing model. These message-passing processes will read all their inputs at the start of their execution and write their outputs at the end of their execution. This technique may result in the overproduction of processes and the techniques of the next chapter may have to be used to reduce the number of processes.

9.3.5 Loops

There is a saying amongst computer scientists that programs spend 90 per cent of their time in 10 per cent of the code: experience suggests this is a conservative estimate. The majority of the time is of course spent within loops, at least with procedural languages. If there is any point in detecting parallelism, the issue of loops must be addressed because this is where there will be the most gain. Indeed, with target architectures based on processor arrays, this will most likely be the only exploitable type of parallelism. Most pipelined processors produce impressive gains in performance when loops are parallelized.

9.3.5.1 Simple Loops

Initially only simple loops are considered; one iteration of the loop is considered to be a process. A simple loop meets the following constraints:

1. Only one variable (the control variable) is used to limit the number of iterations the loop performs.
2. The amount by which the control variable is altered (the step size) is constant.
3. The loop does not exit on a condition.
4. Each iteration only varies in arrays accessed by the control variable plus or minus a constant.
5. Any array accessed by the control variable, is not accessed in any other manner.

A number of assertions can then be about various types of loops:

Total independence

When all assignments within a loop are to members of arrays indexed via the control variable and such arrays are not accessed elsewhere in the loop except via the unmodified control variable, then each iteration of the loop is completely independent of all others. Thus each iteration can be executed in parallel.

Repeated relationship

When all assignments within a loop are to members of arrays indexed via the control variable, plus or minus a constant amount, and such arrays are not accessed elsewhere in the loop except via the control variable (plus or minus a constant), then the relationship between the jth iteration of the loop and the $(k+j)$th is the same as between the ith iteration and the $(k+i)$th (assuming all iterations are within the bounds of the loop). Thus if the usage of a loop is in this manner, then it is only necessary to establish the relationship between the first iteration and other iterations to establish all possible relationships between any iterations of a loop.

By determining the constants used to modify the control variable that access an array, the pattern recurrence between iterations can be established. Thus only the relationships between a few iterations need to be found to determine all the relationships for all iterations.

.5.2 *Nested Loops*

The concept of simple loops can be extended to nested simple loops, where an array can be indexed on several different subscripts. To maintain simplicity it is assumed that any one array will only be indexed in one subscript position by a particular control variable.

Total independence

All iterations of all the loops may be executed in parallel if all assignments are to arrays that are indexed by each of the control variables and none of these arrays are used anywhere else.

Total dependence

For each loop {L1, L2, ..., Ln} that is totally dependent then each of its iterations must be executed sequentially. If all of the nested loops are totally dependent, then all iterations of every loop must be executed sequentially.

Partial dependence

For those nested loops that are not totally dependent it is possible to determine if there is a repeated relationship between iterations, as described previously. This can lead to complicated patterns of interrelationships between iterations of different levels of nesting.

For certain arrays it is possible to detect a *wave front* relationship, which will allow for multi-dimensional interdependencies. For instance, consider the following program fragment:

```
for i←1 to 64 do
    for j←1 to 64 do
        X[i,j]←(X[i−1,j] + X[i,j−1])/2
```

All calculations of values are dependent on the value of X[1,1] being available and there is a fairly complicated interdependencies of the other members of the array X (Figure 9.6). Values of X[0,j] and X[i,0] are used within the loops, but they are not set there and so they don't create further confusion. The propagation by this algorithm of elements that can be calculated is likened to a wave expanding out and hence the name *wave front*.

9.3.6 Using Relationships

Having established the conditions necessary for a particular relationship to exist between two or more processes, it is worth a few words to establish how or what a process is and the approach that can be used to determine the *most parallel form*.

The target hardware will give some guidance to the solution of this thorny problem. It will be necessary to consider the cost of communication between two processes versus the savings gained by executing in parallel. These

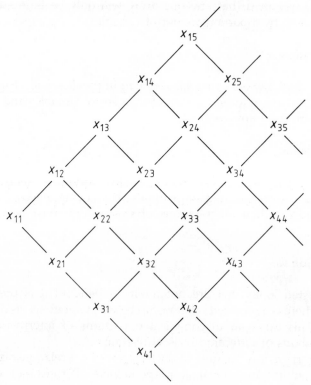

Figure 9.6 *A wave front dependency for* X[i,j]←(X[i−1,,j] + X[i,j−1])/2

figures will vary from architecture to architecture and advances in technologies will certainly have an effect on the results.

3.7 Moving On

Given a relationship is already defined to exist between processes, it is possible to determine if another (more parallel relationship) could be used to link those processes. This situation may arise because the programmer has already indicated that these relationships (or similar ones) exist within the program; alternatively, if a systematic approach is to be made to determining which of these relationships can be said to exist between a set of processes.

In the earlier text it was shown how these relationships could be established for processes that were known to be sequential. Careful examination of the tests shows that the test for Prerequisite includes the test for Conservative, thus having established that some processes could be joined by the Prerequisite relationship they could certainly also be joined by the Conservative relationship. Or to put it the other way, once the Conservative relationship is established, there is less work to do to test if the Prerequisite is also possible.

The Commutative and Contemporary relationships can usually be viewed as alternatives. Both these relationships include the condition for Prerequisite (and by implication Conservative) and so having established that the Prerequisite relationship is possible then there is less work in testing for Commutative or Contemporary. On the other hand, if the Prerequisite relationship is known not to hold then there is no point to testing for Commutative or Contemporary.

3.8 Handling Sequential Programming Constructs

The relationships described so far are amenable to the detection of parallelism in sequential programs consisting only of assignment statements and counted loops. However, programs often consist of other constructs and so any techniques that can be used to increase the number of processes must be able to deal with the commonly used programming constructs.

3.8.1 Conditionals

The conditional statements present an extra difficulty when trying to determine if processes can be executed in parallel, since dependence on the value of a condition may alter the way in which a variable is used. The testing of the value of the condition may involve other variables that may have impact on potential parallelism.

The variables used in the condition will be accessed each time the conditional is executed. However, there will be two different sets of variables used depending on the value of the condition. In trivial cases the value of the condition is known at compile time, but in most programs this is not so. In these non-trivial cases there are two possible approaches that could be taken:

- Assume all the variables in both paths are used
- Introduce conditional parallelism

In the first case the condition is effectively ignored and all variables used lumped together and the appropriate test carried out. This approach will have a number of drawbacks. The parallelism may become very limited and if the conditional encompasses a large amount of code further decomposition may be difficult.

Conditional parallelism appears to be a very attractive idea. For instance, if a condition is true then the statements protected by the conditional can be executed in parallel with process P_i, whereas when the condition is false they may only be executed commutatively.

Dynamic parallelism is not always supported by hardware but the two approaches can be combined to establish a relationship that is acceptable whatever the value of the condition; in the above example that would have to be Commutative.

Maintaining the conditional parallelism may also enable relationships to be established over several conditional statements linked by tests on the same or related variables. Similarly, where conditionals are used to control the number of times a loop is executed, conditionally expressing the parallelism will enable advantage to be taken of more potential parallelism.

9.3.8.2 Procedures

Most programming languages provide a mechanism for calling code defined elsewhere in the program. A variety of namings are used for these facilities: procedures, functions and sub-routines; here just the first is used. Within the body of a procedure three categories of variables can be used:

1. Local variables
2. Global variables
3. Parameters

The effect these categories of variables will have on the potential parallelism between a call of the procedure and surrounding processes will vary. Thus:

1. The local variables will have no effect on parallelism, since by definition they cannot be used anywhere else.
2. The global variables may be used in the external environment and so must be included when determining the relationships between the call and surrounding processes.

3. The variables passed as parameters will vary from call to call of a procedure. The mechanism by which parameters can be passed vary from language to language. A clear understanding of the mechanism is needed if parallelism is to be correctly determined.

Four common mechanisms for parameter passing can be defined:

1. Call-by-value
2. Call-by-reference
3. Copy-restore
4. Call-by-name

For each of these mechanisms it is possible to classify the actual parameters as belonging to one of the groups of variables usage defined earlier.

When a parameter is called by value, the actual parameter is evaluated at call time; any assignments to the formal parameter (if the semantics of the language permit this) will not alter the actual parameter in any way. So where a parameter is called by value it can be associated with the classification W.

A call-by-reference offers a pointer to the actual parameter, so when the formal parameter is changed in the procedure the change occurs to the actual parameter. The consequence of this is that such actual parameters must occur in the appropriate category of variable usage. For instance, if the parameter is only written to, it would be classified as X, while if it were first assigned to and then read, it would be a Z, etc.

Copy-restore can be considered as a cross between the previous two mechanisms. The values are read in at the start of the procedure and copied out at the end, and any intermediate changes are local to the procedure. There are striking similarities between this mechanism and that of processors with private memories. Any variables passed by this mechanism can be categorized as Y according to usage, although there may be cases where another category was sufficient.

Call-by-name is the approach used when expanding macros. At compile time the body of the procedure is substituted for the call and the formal parameters replaced by the actual ones. In this case the obvious approach is to assume the macro expansion and treat the detection of parallelism in the same manner as with other pieces of sequential code.

3.9 Additional Considerations

In the previous sections a number of the most commonly used programming constructs have been considered and consideration given as to how they aid or hinder the detection of parallelism. Data structures have not been considered although there is obviously potential for the exploitation of parallelism between different parts of the structure. A possible approach would be to identify components of a compound structure (e.g. fields of a record) as independent variables and then *parallelize* loops performing operations on the whole structure.

The dreaded **goto** provides few headaches when detecting parallelism: if it is possible to determine all implications of where a **goto** goes, then it can just be treated as a reordering of code.

Input and output need to be handled with care if unexpected events are not to occur. A process must ensure that what it reads is intended for it and two processes should not (normally) attempt to write to the same part of a display unit.

In general the detection of parallelism should take place as part of the compilation process. There is an argument that says the compilation process itself should be the subject of *parallelizing*.

9.4   VECTORIZING COMPILERS

The programmer is sometimes relieved of the need to think about potential parallelism, by the use of compilers that introduce parallelism. Such compilers are most frequently associated with pipelined and processor arrays. Such compilers are known as vectorizing compilers because they introduce parallelism into operations on arrays, usually one dimension at a time, and one-dimensional arrays are sometimes known as vectors.

A typical vectorizing compiler takes a code written in a sequential language (frequently Fortran) and generates machine code for the parallel target architecture, the machine code indicating as many parallel operations as possible. This is normally achieved by template matching [Hockney and Jesshope 1988]. Loops of constant bounds and step size operating solely on elements of arrays indexed by the control variable can easily be detected and vectorized. For example:

```
    DO label X = 1 TO 64
label: ARRAY1 (X) = ARRAY1 (X) + ARRAY2 (X)
```

could be matched to machine-code statements for pipelining addition or simultaneously adding 64 elements of arrays on a processor array.

More complicated operations can also have templates constructed:

- Loops where the bounds don't match the parallelism of the architecture
- Loops with variable bounds
- Conditionals
- Procedure calls
- Nested constructs

In general these approaches are similar to the ones mentioned earlier for detecting parallelism.

Although vectorizing compilers start from sequential code they are not able to introduce parallelism in all cases. Some constructs are inherently unsuitable for parallelizing, others are difficult for the vectorizer to analyse. Thus although the programmer does not need to use parallel constructs there is a need to understand how the vectorizing compiler works. Where code is amenable to parallelism being found, the programmer must present it in the correct manner, and constructs not amenable to parallel implementation should be avoided. For instance, few vectorizing compilers will reorder loops, so the dependencies should be in the innermost loops so that the potential parallelism will be found in the outermost loops.

REDUCING PARALLELISM

When there are more processes representing the solution to a problem than there are physical processors, then it may be necessary to map several processes on to a single processor or to reduce the number of processes.

> Poor old Mum left to do the washing-up on her own, she will have to take all the tasks normally performed by the rest of the family and do them herself.

The mapping of many processes onto a single processor can be likened to running a multi-user environment on a conventional sequential machine. In a multi-user environment decisions must be taken as to which work to do next: care must be taken to ensure integrity of data, etc. Similarly with multi-processes mapped on to a single processor there is a need to decide which process (or part of one) should be executed next, to protect the private data, etc. The problem is made somewhat more complex if there is more than one processor (but still insufficient) for executing the processes required. Occam on the transputer successfully uses this approach, thus allowing a many-process program to run on a single transputer, even to give the appearance of synchronous message-passing. When there is more than one processor that the processes can be executed on the onus is on the user to define the configuration of the software onto the physical resource.

An alternative to mapping several processes on to a single processor and then multiprogramming, is to consider that a number of processes can be merged into a single process, which can be then executed on a single processor. This may result in considerable alterations to the code. For instance, variables may need to be renamed to avoid naming conflicts. Any communication between merged processes will have to be treated differently. For instance, where one process calculates a value V which another process expects to be sent and will store the value in L, then the whole communication will be replaced by a simple assignment of *V* to *L*. However, it does avoid the problems of how to synchronize a number of processes that are on a single processor.

The exact way in which parallelism can be removed will depend on the model of parallelism. Some programs, especially those that rely on all processors simultaneously carrying an operation, will create severe difficulties when attempts are made to sequentialize them.

9.5.1   Merging Processor Array Processes

Most processor array languages require that the parallelism is closely linked to that of the hardware architecture. As a result, array processing parallelism is rarely used to express natural parallelism; more likely *exploitable* parallelism. The problem is mapped in terms of the number of processors available rather than a form *natural* to the designer. Thus the main motivation for changing the number of processes will be when transporting to a different sized architecture, for example, moving from a 64×64 processor array to a 32×32 architecture. Thus the general case can be considered to be reducing the number of processes by a multiple of two.

> At the holiday cottage the number of identical mindless clones for washing up is maybe a quarter of those available at home. The allocation of work and the instructions issued by the boss will have to be altered to take account of the decrease in the staff available.

Two approaches can once again be taken: either mapping several processes on to one processor or merging several processes into one new process. In either case it is necessary to decide which processes to group together. The main problems in planning these mergers will be when all the processes were expected to calculate values simultaneously and pass them around. So essentially both approaches will need to be given the same consideration. Here emphasis will be placed on merging several processes into one, and, in passing, it will be mentioned that these techniques will be of use when mapping several processes onto a single processor.

9.5.2   Merging Pipelined Processes

The nature of a pipeline dictates that the first processor completes the first task and passes information on to the second processor, which will then use this information in its computation. Thus two adjacent processes could be merged onto one processor by ensuring that the computation of the first process is performed first followed by the second, and then the first again, etc. Several problems may be forecast with this type of merging:

1. Specialist hardware is not available to support the new process.
2. Iterations of a process rely on intermediate result.
3. The new process becomes a bottleneck.

The ways in which these problems will be overcome will depend on the motivation for merging the processes in the first place.

1. If separate units are available for different arithmetic operations then it is only possible to merge those adjacent processes that perform the same operation. In exceptional cases it may be deemed acceptable to transform one operation to another (for example, a multiplication may be replaced by a number of adds).
2. Careful consideration as to the naming of variables will avoid any loss of results that could be required in future iterations on this process. This problem is addressed again when considering message passing.
3. If two processes are merged then it is reasonable to assume that the new process will take (approximately) twice as long. If the original pipeline was carefully balanced and these were the only two processes merged, then the resultant process would indeed create a bottleneck that would halve the performance of the system. However, if all the processes in the pipeline were to be merged to create a program for a sequential processor, then this would not be a problem. Similarly, if two *short* processes were chosen to be merged or there was an overall reduction in the number of processes.

5.3 Merging Shared Memory Processes

Within a shared memory environment it is fairly straightforward to merge two processes. There is a slight complication when processors are considered to have private memory available. In the case when there is no private memory the methodology for transforming two processes into one will be: if an ordering is dictated then it will be maintained, if no ordering is dictated then impose an arbitrary one. For example, two processes that could be executed in parallel will probably be transformed into the code of the second followed by the code of the first.

Where private memory is used to maintain local copies of variables for a process, this facility will have to be simulated in the merged process. Variables that would be used in both processes will be given a local name in each of the constituent parts. At the end of the new process the values in the two parts will have to be brought together in the manner dictated by the original relationship linking the two processes. Essentially the value could be:

1. That originally in the variable before either process used it.
2. The value set by the first process.
3. The value set by the second process.
4. A non-deterministic value.

9.5.4   Merging simple Message-passing Processes

Consider two processes P1 and P2 that communicate with each other once only via a channel C12. For simplicity it is assumed that information flows from process P1 to P2 and that there is no reverse flow, that is in a pipeline fashion. Also P1 and P2 will not contain any loops.

It is essential, for this merger to be successful, that the same name is not used in both processes. Thus the first step will be a simple renaming, each variable can be prefixed by a unique processor identifier.

It is necessary to match the output of an expression by P1

(i.e. C12 ! *expr*)

by the inputting of the value to a variable within P2

(i.e. C12 ? *var*)

This pair of statements will be replaced by a single new assignment, of the form:

var : = *expr*

For ease of explanation in the next sentences it will be assumed that those statements in P1 that occur before the output to C12 are sub-process P11 and all those that occur after are sub-process P12. Similarly, all the statements in P2 that occur before the input from C12 are sub-process P21 and all those that occur after are sub-process P22.

All the statements in P11 must occur before the new assignment in the composite process, and those in P12 must appear after. Similarly, all the statements in P21 must occur before the new assignment in the composite process, and those in P22 must appear after. However, there are no constraints about how the statements of P1 and P2 are merged (other than in relationship to the new assignment). This merging may be achieved in the same manner as described for shared memory.

9.5.5   Merging More Complicated Message-passing Processes

In the previous section very simple merges were considered; here a tinge of reality is introduced.

.5.1 Bi-directional Communication

If the previous example is expanded to allow for a second communication from P2 to P1 via a channel C21, then there will have to be expansions to the techniques for merging the two processes. Renaming will be required as before. Then it will be necessary to determine the temporal ordering of the use of the two channels. The ordering must be the same in both processes, otherwise the program is faulty and would deadlock. The remainder of both processes can then be labelled as sub-processes (P11, P12, P13 and P21, P22, P23), sub-processes P12 and P22 representing the statements that will be executed between the two communications in their respective processes.

i.e.

P11	P21
C12 ! a+b	
	C12 ? v
P12	P22
C21 ? y	
	C21 ! c+d
P13	P23

The two communications can then be replaced by the appropriate assignments. The sub-processes P11 and P21 are merged, as described earlier, to appear before the assignment. The sub-processes P12 and P22 are merged to appear between the two assigments. Finally the sub-processes P13 and P23 are merged and placed after the second assignment.

.5.2 Communications via Several Channels

The above can easily be expanded to allow for any number of channels, and for several communications via a single channel.

.5.3 Guarded Communications

Communications are sometimes protected with guards. This will mean that it is not always easy to pair a particular output on a channel with an input on the same channel. Thus the guard mechanism has to be maintained even in the sequential composite process or perhaps simulated via conditionals.

.5.4 Loops

When the two processes are controlled by a looping structure the merged process will almost certainly also be controlled by a loop. Before attempting to merge the two loops they must both conform to the same structure. For instance, if the first communication of the loop in P1 is an output to channel C12, then the first communication of P2's loop is an input from channel C12. This may only be achieved by unrolling and refolding the loop.

9.5.6 Incidental Optimizations

The techniques described so far for all the models have maintained the majority of the original processes' statements. The time taken to execute the combined processes will be in the region of twice that on two processes.[1]

It may be possible to optimize the resultant process and to minimize the time needed. Each of the processes resulting from a merge can be subject to optimizations in the same manner as any sequential program. In particular there may be redundancies present because of the evaluation on separate processors, which after merging can be eliminated. For instance, when two message passing processes are merged, an output by process P1 of a value X to a variable V in process P2, will result in an assignment:

$$V := X$$

If V is never reset then all subsequent references to V can be replaced by X, and the above assignment discarded.

9.5.7 CSP and Occam

Occam is based on the communicating sequential process (CSP) concept. Thus the sound semantic base of CSP can also be seen in occam. It is possible to develop rules or laws for occam programming and to show the semantic equivalence of two different representations of the same occam program [Roscoe and Hoare 1986]. Thus occam is an ideal medium for development of automatic transformations from one parallel form to another.

---

[1]This is necessarily a rule-of-thumb calculation: the figures may be very similar if the original processes were designed in such a way that they were constantly waiting for the other to communicate.

9.6   CHAPTER REVIEW

- The extremes of altering the number of processes are represented by:
  —transforming a sequential program into a parallel one
  —transforming a parallel program into a sequential one
- Studying tree representations of program structures will reveal parallelism
- Manipulating tree structures may provide more potential parallelism
- Studying the usage and flow of data will also reveal potential parallelism
- Parallel processes can be merged to produce sequential versions.

10 *Changing the Model*

Once a problem has been programmed it holds some value related to the amount of work invested in achieving it. Often it is considered to be *cheaper* to massage an existing program to fit a new architecture than to redesign it to match the new model. In this chapter, ways in which such a transportation can be achieved will be highlighted.

There is no implication that this is the best way to solve the problems of parallelism. Rather it is an attempt to show ways in which some of the problems of swapping parallel architectures can be overcome.

In the longer term, problems will probably be better solved completely independently of any parallel architecture and then mapped down onto the most appropriate (or available) one. To a certain extent this is what is offered by the object-oriented and functional approaches, described in Chapter 7.

In the previous chapter consideration was given as to how a program could be made more or less parallel. The model of parallelism remained unaltered, except when the special case of only one process was considered. Of course using one process is the representation of a sequential programming model. If it is required to change programming models then there may well be a need to consider altering the number of processes as well: that need is not discussed in detail here.

For instance, the family may replace the children's efforts at dishwashing by a group of mindless clones.

Or some of the infant children may grow up to be Professors.

When it is required to transport a program working under one model to a new environment, there are essentially three approaches:

1. Transform the program according to a set of guidelines or rules for changing from model *A* to model *B*.

2. Transform the program into an intermediate form and from there change it to suit the target model.

3. Backtrack on the development path of the original solution to the point where the architectural choice was made and then take the new track.

The third is perhaps the most realistic from the software engineering viewpoint; however, this information may not be available. When new parallel processing notations are developed it would be useful if they were able to be architecturally independent.

The use of an intermediate form would reduce the number of translation systems that have to be designed. However, care will be needed to avoid potential parallelism becoming blurred when transporting between two similar models via an unsympathetic intermediate form.

In this chapter both approaches will be discussed, including some proposals for intermediate forms and some techniques for direct translation, when this is appropriate.

10.1   INTERMEDIATE FORMS

The problems of transporting serial programs from one machine to another are well known [Brown 1977]. One approach is to develop a translator from each language to each target machine, or to a language executable on that machine (Figure 10.1). Where several languages and machines are considered this can lead to a large number of translators requiring to be written. A classic solution to this problem is to use an abstract machine or an intermediate form as an intermediary for all transportation (Figure 10.2).

Given six possible models each of which are required to be mapped on to each other, then if one translator is to be written for each pair then thirty translators would be needed, whereas if there was a suitable intermediate form only twelve translators would be required (six into the intermediate form and six out).

Similar arguments can be used for transporting programs between models of parallelism. The big problem is designing the intermediate form to be a good medium for all models. As yet there is no intermediate form presented that will enable transportation between all the models presented in this text, although there is an obvious technique that will be presented in the next section.

10.1.1   Sequential Intermediate Form

In the previous chapter consideration was given as to how the amount of parallelism in a representation could be increased or decreased. The ultimate forms of these are to

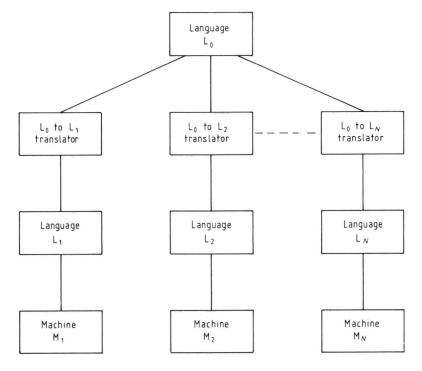

Figure 10.1 *Translation from one language to many machines*

- introduce parallelism into a sequential form, or
- to remove all parallelism, producing a sequential form

For many languages and models these two areas are well researched. There is often a need to produce sequential versions of code when software development takes place away from the target. From a marketing point of view it is advantageous to offer a 'parallelizing' interpreter, as this allows customers to believe they will not need to rewrite existing programs.

There are a couple of flaws in the above argument:

1. Rather than necessarily producing sequential code, code is sometimes tested on a simulator.
2. When sequential code is produced it is often optimized, so that it will execute reasonably well on the single processor. Thus potential parallelism will be lost.

> This is possibly akin to trying to stick together six glasses, after the tray they were on was dropped on the kitchen floor.

However, the idea is attractive and should not be lightly dismissed.

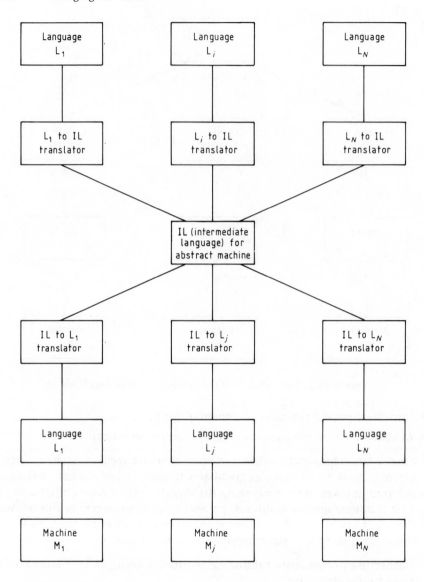

Figure 10.2 *Translation of* N *languages to each other via an intermediate form*

To try and evade the loss of potential parallelism it is suggested here that the translation from the source into the sequential form is *sloppy*. That is, the sequential code produced pays no attention to performance, efficiency, etc.; it merely is a sequential representation of the original problem. The second part of the transportation operation will be where the emphasis is on producing some form of optimal code. See Figure 10.3.

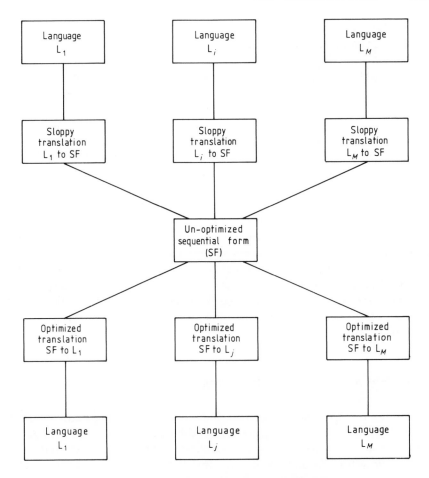

Figure 10.3 *A sequential intermediate language*

Grandmother has a rough plan of how she will tackle the housework if she has to do the job on her own. But she is amenable to dividing the work between any helpers who may present themselves.

Indeed, she is able to cope with helpers with different abilities: Grandfather is capable of cleaning the windows on his own, but the children need to be supervised while they dust.

Production of such a model for portability will require very little effort. The translators to the *sloppy* sequential forms will have to be written, but as these will be a verbatim translation they should not require too much effort. The second-part translators should be already available from the manufacturers of the target hardware and so will not require to be written at all.

10.1.2   Parallel Computer Systems for Integrating Numeric and Symbolic Processing (SPAN)

The ESPRIT-funded SPAN project aims to investigate programming languages and parallel architectures for the integration of symbolic and numeric processing. A virtual machine is defined that will facilitate the mapping of the languages onto machines. All languages are to be transformed into the virtual machine code which can then be mapped onto the required parallel architecture for execution. The architectures that are considered by this project are all of a large-grained nature, essentially either message passing or shared memory, although there is an object-oriented architecture, which is in fact emulated on top of transputers. Processor arrays or pipeline processors are not considered as part of this project.

The virtual machine is based on the work of Refenes [1987], who identified the major architectural mechanisms in symbolic and numeric languages. This led to the definition of a *general-purpose* architecture that allowed representation of both paradigms. This model is embodied into a programming language and its associated virtual machine, which can be mapped onto one of the target architectures or can be realized as an *ideal* parallel machine.

10.1.3   Portable Array and Pipeline Programs

Even when transporting within a single model there are still all the problems associated with the subtle differences in the underlying architectures (just as in the conventional serial case). In an attempt to overcome these difficulties and to allow transformation of programs for processor arrays to pipeline form (and vice versa), Williams [1979] proposed an approach based on an intermediate form.

Using the proposed approach an *abstract machine* is defined, which can be programmed in an *intermediate language*. The architecture of the abstract machine will affect the ease or difficulty with which the translation process can take place. The architecture of the abstract machine is chosen so as to be amenable to the type of problems for which the two models are usually used. The main motivation for using either pipelined processors or processor arrays is that they are good at performing operations on large quantities of data in the form of arrays. Thus the abstract machine must also be capable of performing operations on arrays. This leads to one of three designs:

1. The *ideal machine*
2. The *maximum machine*
3. The *minimum machine*

An ideal machine seems the perfect solution; however, determining what this is is extremely difficult (although for a slightly different set of criteria the SPAN project does attempt to do this). The maximum machine would represent all the array operations that currently have been defined (plus any ones likely to be defined in the near future). This would produce a large abstract machine containing many similar properties. The most attractive model is the minimum machine that contains only simple array operations, which like *building blocks* can be used to produce any of the possible operations.

2 ARRAY–PIPELINE PROCESSES

As explained earlier, there are many levels at which pipelining may be introduced. Instruction and lower levels of pipelining are used (in general) to obtain a better performance from a sequential program. Programs are not (usually) *written* to take advantage of this parallelism, rather the compiler takes a sequential program and produces optimized code for this particular architecture. Thus for these target architectures the problem would be the same as that discussed in Chapter 9 (namely, making a sequential program run on a processor array architecture or a processor array program run on a sequential architecture).

Macro-pipelining is more amenable to programmer exploitation of the parallelism, although in some cases this will still be left to the compiler (the so-called *vectorizing compilers*), which again degenerates into the sequential case mentioned above. Transformation from a program suited to a processor array into a program for a macro-pipeline processor should be a simple task, as the parallelism will be of a similar granularity, although there may be difficulties in avoiding bottlenecks within the pipeline. Complicated data dependencies will serve to make the transformation difficult, and care will need to be taken that the correct version of a frequently updated array is used in the version transformed to.

The reverse transformation may cause some problems due to the finite number of processing elements in the target processor array as opposed to the variable number of tasks that may pass through the pipeline.

> In the dishwashing scenario, these transformations can be likened to the family swapping between the conventional pipeline and the array of mindless clones.

A high-level specification of a problem with a number of operations on arrays should be amenable to solution on processor arrays and pipeline processors. The language Actus and the proposed Fortran standard allow programs to be written for both array and pipeline processors. Thus a program written in such a language could be run on either type of processor without any need for transformations.

In general programs for processor arrays take the form:

```
FOR ALL i←1 TO N DO
    A[i]
    B[i]
    C[i]
```

All the statements of the form $A[i]$ are executed simultaneously on different processing elements of the processor array. When these are complete all the $B[i]$ statements are executed and then the $C[i]$. A version for a three-processor pipeline would in the jth cycle be calculating $A[j]$ on the first processor, $B[j-1]$ on the second processor and $C[j-2]$ on the third. This would not be a correct transformation if statement $C[i]$ used a value in $A[k]$ or $B[k]$ (with $k>i$), as the new values would not be available yet; similarly, $B[i]$ should not expect all values in A to be available. There is also a danger that $A[i]$ will reference a value in $C[m]$ (with $m<i$) where the value in $C[i]$ has been prematurely updated.

A study of the usage of variables would reveal such dependencies: simple dependencies should not defeat the transformation. For instance, if the only interdependency in the loop was that $C[i]$ used a value calculated in $A[k]$ where $(k>i)$, then the pipeline could be started with the control variable at N and decremented down to 1. In fact the pipeline could receive any one of the possible values of the control variable as its first task; the second and subsequent tasks would be chosen from the remaining possible values. However, there will be degenerate cases that are not mappable. Such programs will have to be executed sequentially if the processor array were to be replaced by a pipeline (or the user may be invited to consider rewriting the code—the dependency may not be critically dependent on whether it is the current, next or previous value of a particular variable).

All the above statements are equally relevant to the transformation from code for a pipeline processor onto a processor array. The other problems that will be faced when transforming between the two models will stem from a mis-match between the processes and the number of processors.

The fragment of program above will probably be best executed on an array processor with N processing elements or a pipeline processor with three (i.e. the number of statements) processors. Thus there will be two aspects to this transformation:

1. Changing the model.
2. Fitting on to the available number of processors.

Changing the model is described above, and in the new model fitting the number of processes to the number of processors is discussed previously.

For instance, if the above fragment was to be converted to run on an architecture with six possible pipes, then assuming there were no complicating data dependencies, the change to a pipeline version would be straightforward. To take advantage of all the available processors would require the spreading of the three processes to fit onto the six processors: this may be as simple as splitting each of the processes into two or there may be a need to balance the work so that no processor becomes (too much of) a bottleneck.

.3 SHARED MEMORY–MESSAGE PASSING

Basically the two models of parallelism provided by the shared memory and the message-passing models are very similar.

The difference stems from the privacy of data.
- In a shared-memory environment specific measures must be taken to protect delicate data.
- In a message-passing environment steps need to be taken to share data needed by more than one process.

The difference is that of the family having a single table, on which everyone places dishes and has the ability to remove dishes, compared with every member of the family having their own personal table that only they can use.

In both cases there are the usual procedural operations in addition to operations for expressing parallelism. The problems of changing the syntax to be correct for the target model are interesting, but do not relate specifically to the use of parallelism. The important factor in such transformations is to verify that the semantics of both sets of syntaxes are identical. The same can be said for the operations that express parallelism, for instance there will be a direct mapping between the semantics of a FORK statement and a PAR, so that change will be quickly undertaken.

The most challenging part of this transformation is to provide the facilities used by one model and not available in another. In particular, the shared-memory model passes information from one process to another via common variables whereas the message-passing model explicitly sends values across channels shared between two processes. The shared-memory model can be further divided into models with and without private memory attached to each processor. With private memory being used, the only points where information can be passed to the other processes is at the end of the process. This makes for very easy rules of transformation, so that case will be addressed first.

For each of the shared-memory processes it is possible to list those variables that need to be supplied to a process and those which are changed by a process. It is also possible to provide a temporal ordering on the processes, by studying the operations that provide parallelism and sequentiality. Thus the flow of data can be determined.

The end of each shared-memory process will need to have appended a series of outputs and the start will need a series of inputs so that it can become a message-passing process. For example, consider a process P0 containing the following:

```
:
a←3
b←72
:
```

If this is transformed from a shared memory environment the message passing form will need to send the values of *a* and *b* to any processes that need to use them. The outputs will take the form of a communication to each other process that uses a value created in this process. For example:

> send value of a to P1, P3, P5

and

> send value of b to P1, P2, P6

The inputs will take the form of a communication from each of the other processes that provide a value used in this process. The communication will read the values at the beginning of this process of all variables shared between these two processes. Process P1 (in the message-passing form) will start with:

> receive a from P0

and

> receive b from P0

When the shared-memory model does not provide the protection of private memory, the transformation is a little more difficult. Simply what is needed is that every shared variable is allocated to a particular process that will provide access to it.

The first step will be to identify all variables that are shared between different processes. Then each variable must be allocated to a specific process, in one of two ways:

1. Place each shared variable within one of the processes, called its *caretaker*, and require all other processes to access it by passing messages to its caretaker. This requires that the caretaker exists as long as the shared variable is in use.
2. Alternatively, a new process can be introduced for each shared variable (or set of shared variables). This new process will act as a *monitor*. All processes accessing the shared variable do so via the monitor.

The first approach has the advantage of not increasing the number of processes; however, in all but the most trivial of cases it will be impossible to predict when the caretaker will be requested to provide access to a variable in its care. Thus the only solution may be at every statement to poll the other processes to identify any that may require access. This constant polling may well detract from the performance of the new process.

The second approach will not significantly alter the body of each process in the computation, but it will need the creation of a number of new monitor processes. As with the caretaker, the monitor will need to be constantly vigilant, waiting for a request to access a variable. However, in this case the facility will not be at the cost of performance, except for any loss associated with increasing the number of processes.

Example

Consider the following three processes:

Process P1
    temp1←x × x

Process P2
    temp2←y × y

Process P3
    result←temp1 + temp2

If these are linked together (in a shared-memory environment) by the following parallel operators:

```
:
FORK P1, P2
JOIN P1, P2
P3
```

then what is the message-passing equivalent?

- Process P1 will have to read in the value of x, from wherever it is set, and forward the value of temp1 to process P3 where it is needed
- Similarly, P2 will read in y, and forward temp2
- Process P3 will receive the values of temp1 and temp2 from processes P1 and P2 (in some order) and the result will be forwarded somewhere

Thus the message-passing equivalent could be (in occam-like notation):

```
SEQ
    PAR
        P1'
        P2'
    P3'
```

where the processes P1', P2' and P3' are defined as:

```
PROCESS P1'                        PROCESS P2'
    SEQ                                SEQ
        somewhere.1 ? x                    somewhere.2 ? y
        temp1←x × x                        temp2←y × y
        toP3.1 ! temp1                     toP3.2 ! temp2


    PROCESS P3'
        SEQ
            PAR
                toP3.1 ? temp1
                toP3.2 ? temp2
            result←temp1 + temp2
            anywhere ! result
```

This could then be optimized in a number of ways. The synchronization of P3' with P1' and P2' need not be done explicitly, as it will result from the passing of the values of temp1 and temp2. Assignments to variables which immediately pass their values out (without any subsequent use) can be merged to a single output of a calculated sum.

The macros described in Chapter 5 that allowed the writing of portable programs for shared-memory architectures have been adapted to allow programs to run on some message-passing architectures. Programs written using these macros can be implemented on both message-passing and shared-memory architectures. However, it is recommended that *different programming styles* are used to suit the target architecture.

10.3.1   Message Passing to Shared Memory

The conversion from the message-passing model to shared memory can benefit from the similarities between the two models in the same way as the reverse transformation. To prevent any name clashes it would be wise to introduce a naming policy that provides a different name on each process. For instance, each variable could be suffixed by the name of the owner process. Once again the approach will be different depending on whether the shared-memory model has local private memory for use by each process.

The use of private memory effectively debars any communication between processes. Thus wherever a message-passing process requires to input or output variables it will be necessary to split the process, so that the input is at the start of the new process or the output at the end of the new process. A modification to the naming policy will have to be introduced to ensure that the value output can be read by the appropriate processes.

When private memory is not used it will not be necessary to fragment processes, although the approach may in some cases offer the best solution. An alternative approach is to use a synchronization mechanism such as flags to protect the integrity of a message that would formerly have been passed. The message can then become an assignment of the value calculated in the outputting process to the variable in the input process. The assignment can be resident in either process, the synchronization mechanism providing appropriate protection [Ben-Ari 1982].

Care must be taken when transforming from a synchronous message-passing language that uses parallel operators (such as PAR) and provides synchronization via the passing of messages. It is easy to forget about one kind of parallelism/sequencing, but both must be considered when a correct transformation is to be obtained.

Example

Consider the following:

```
PAR
    SEQ
        intosq1 ? x
        outtoadd1 ! x × x
    SEQ
        intosq2 ? y
        outtoadd2 ! y × y
    SEQ
        PAR
            outtoadd1 ? r
            outtoadd2 ? s
        result ! r + s
```

The three parts of the program joined by SEQs can be transformed into the following three processes:

```
                    PROCESS P1
                        temp.1←x.1 × x.1
    PROCESS P2
        temp.2←y.1 × y.1
                                        PROCESS P3
                                            result.3←temp.1 + temp.2
```

The first two processes can still be executed in parallel. However, there is a hidden sequencing with the third process in the message-passing model, as it cannot proceed until the values of *r* or *s* are offered. Thus in a shared-memory environment this will have to be explicitly sequentialized, giving the following relationships between the processes:

```
SEQ
    PAR
        P1
        P2
    P3
```

10.4 OTHER MODELS TO CONCRETE REALIZATIONS

In Chapter 7 a number of models were introduced that did not mirror hardware architectures (although in some cases work is progressing on hardware realizations of these models). In this section techniques for mapping some of these models onto some of the models based on hardware are discussed.

10.4.1 Applicative to Shared Memory or Array Processor

An applicative program annotated with potential parallelism is an ideal candidate for mapping onto a number of processes linked to a single shared memory. This would mean that there would be no need to copy the values read by the individual processes as all values would be globally available: results can be gathered in as they become available. The only potential disadvantage with this approach is that the granularity of the parallelism may be very small (say adding two integers). So (somewhat surprisingly) the processor array model may be a better target. The halfsum calculation of Chapter 7 becomes a large number of additions, many of which can take place simultaneously.

The recipe to be followed is to unwrap the recursion of the applicative program to the lowest level. As long as these are all linked by similar operations, this becomes a single iteration of the processor array, once the data are made available to the appropriate processors. The recursion can then be rolled back up to provide more iterations, each using less of the processing elements. Thus halfsum defined in Chapter 7 to be:

```
fun sum n = halfsum (1,n)
fun halfsum (low, high) =
          if (high = low) then high
          else halfsum (low, mid) + halfsum (mid + 1, high)
          where mid = (low + high) div 2
```

With the **else** clause appropriately marked as potentially parallel, this could be unwound and folded again to give:

```
for i←1 to n/2 step 1
    for j←1 to n − i step i
        a [j]←a [j] + a [j + i]
```

More complicated conditionals will require the use of masking on some processing elements.

0.4.2 Dataflow to Message Passing

To transform a program represented by a dataflow model to a message-passing representation requires the identification of sequences which represent the values that have the property of occurring exactly once as a left-hand side of an equation and elsewhere as the right-hand side of an equation (or equations): these are the values that can be passed through the channels.

It is also required that apart from communication through these special 'channel' variables, the equations must separate into groups that use disjoint sets of variables. This may result in a variable having several different versions–one for each process it is used in. It is also necessary to correctly sequence the actions within a process to ensure the resulting message-passing processes are correct and sequential.

Example

Consider the dataflow representation of a very simple polynomial function:

$$V = a_0 + U \times (a_1 + U \times a_2)$$

For simplicity it is assumed that that there is an infinite number of inputs and consequently outputs. The problem can be segmented to produce the following dataflow (Lucid-like) program:

(1) $U = input$
(2) $output = a_0 + U \times Y$
(3) $Y = a_1 + U \times a_2$

To be in keeping with the original definition of the problem the input is called U and the output V. The two lines of the program (2) and (3) are equivalent to message-passing processes, that can be labelled (A) and (B), respectively:

$$V = a_0 + U \times Y \tag{A}$$
$$Y = a_1 + U \times a_2 \tag{B}$$

A diagrammatic representation of these two processes is given in Figure 10.4.

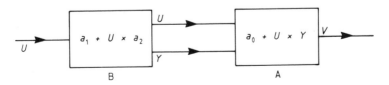

Figure 10.4 *Message-passing representation of a simple polynomial function*

It can easily be determined that the sequence Y occurs exactly once as a left-hand side, in process (B), and once in a right-hand side, in process (A). This needs to be replaced by a channel communication. To illustrate the direction of flow the channel will be labelled chAB, so processes (A) and (B) become;

chAB? y $V = a_0 + U \times y$ (A)
  chAB! $(a_1 + U \times a_2)$ (B)

Note at this point the ordering of statements within processes is not considered; V can be replaced in the same manner giving:

chAB? y   chV!$a_0 + U \times y$ (A)
  chAB!$(a_1 + U \times a_2)$ (B)

Channel chV communicates with the *outside world*, i.e. it allows process (A) to emit data from the pipeline.

The sequence U is used in both processes so it will be necessary to replicate its values. The values of U will be introduced into the pipeline by a channel chU, which will link (B) with the outside world. chuAB will be used to pass the values of U, along to process A, giving:

chuAB?uA chAB? y chV!$(a_0 + uA \times y)$ (A)
chU?u chAB!$(a_1 + u \times a_2)$ chuAB!u   (B)

Having established the operations within the processes it is now necessary to establish the sequence in which operations can take place. A number of orderings are possible, but the interaction between two processes must be considered. In particular, when more than one channel links two processes the order in which the channels are used must be the same for both processes. Thus an arbitrary correct ordering can be chosen for both processes.

chuAB?uA;chAB?y;chV!$a_0 + uA \times y$
chU?u;chuAB!u;chAB!$(a_1 + u \times a_2)$

10.4.3 Logic Programming to Message Passing

Techniques similar to the ones described above can be used to map logic programs onto a message-passing model, or the intermediate form of the SPAN project could be used. Lacking a special-purpose architecture, the message-passing model will offer the most appropriate base, with which a tree structure, as described in the previous chapter, can be readily modelled.

0.5 CHAPTER REVIEW

- The programming model can be changed:
  — via an intermediate form
  — directly
- The intermediate form requires only a small number of translators, but the representation of the intermediate is difficult
  — one solution is to use a sequential intermediate form
- It is relatively easy to transform between some models, e.g.
  — processor arrays and pipelines
  — message passing and shared memory
- In other cases the difficulties favour the use of an intermediate form.

11 Summary, Conclusions and the Future

In this book a number of different programming models for parallel processing systems have been described along with the problems associated with changing the model. There are three questions that this work begs:

1. Why use parallelism?
2. Why are there so many models of parallelism?
3. Why attempt to alter the model?

1.1 WHY USE PARALLELISM?

There are three possible motivations for using a parallel processor:

1. It's the available architecture
2. To achieve a required performance
3. Because the underlying problem is inherently parallel.

The first point is the one that has been addressed in this book: here's an architecture, how can it be used? There are many attractions in this point of view.

The moulding of problems on to an existing architecture is a task that is faced over and over again within computer science. The problems that have been addressed here are to give a general class of architectures and show how the class can be used. The specific examples are given only to provide guidance as to the general use of the class, not to provide the reader with a course in how to program that machine, or even to discuss the relevant merits of different manufacturers' products. Hopefully these models will be relevant long after the particular architectures have been superseded.

Performance is an issue that some of us choose to ignore at this stage, although others will argue that a non-functional requirement such as performance must be considered right from the first specification.

The natural parallelism in a problem is an area which I regret does not fit well into this book. The area is alluded to when transformations are mentioned, but it is an area that must be developed if parallel processing is really to escape from the idiosyncrasies of particular hardwares. Indeed, the whole issue of specification of parallelism needs much further investigation [Ibrahim et al 1989].

11.2   WHY SO MANY MODELS OF PARALLELISM?

In the early part of this book a number of different models of parallelism were introduced. This begs the question of why is there more than one model of parallelism. Surely, if a problem can be solved so that the work is divided between a number of processors then that is the parallel form. The difficulties come from the immense differences between the underlying hardware architectures. Some offer potential for thousands of parallel processes but they must all perform the same simple instructions, while others allow independent operation between a relatively few processors. For instance, matrix multiplication has been shown [Quinn 1987] to be best represented as outer product, middle product or inner product depending on the target parallel architecture.

A study of a single model of parallelism may have disguised the need to choose different algorithms depending on the nature of the underlying hardware and, additionally which model would have been chosen. There are many models of parallelism to reflect the variety of architectures available. There are opportunities to present models that are not dependent on the architecture–but these are not representative of all the hardware models.

11.3   WHY ATTEMPT TO ALTER THE MODEL?

If what is said above is acceptable (that is, there are a variety of parallel models), then one motivation for changing the model is that the underlying hardware has changed. Two approaches are possible for changing between models:

1. A direct translation from one to the other.

2. Translation via an intermediate form.

In an ideal world translations would be fully automatic (like a compiler) but at the current state of the art such translations are much more likely to be done with human interaction.

.4 A FUTURE FOR PARALLEL PROGRAMMING

If writing parallel programs is to progress from the black-art phase to the *engineering* phase, there is a need for methods to be developed that will support the development of parallel software for one or more target parallel architectures. The possibility of methods for parallel programming is currently under investigation for limited domains. There is a need for these domains to be expanded to include all problems and target architectures. There is also a need for tools to be available to support the design and development of parallel solutions. Again some exist, but are not general purpose or sufficient to cover all needs.

An alternative route that should be addressed at the same time is an investigation into the possibility of defining an ideal machine that is mappable onto all real parallel hardwares. Some attempts to achieve this have been made in the second part of this book. A more realistic goal may be to define a maximum machine that encompasses all the different models of parallelism. There is a great deal of work to be done before either of these can be realized in a usable form.

There is much work still to be done in the field of parallel processing.

Bibliography

Ackerman, William B. 1982 'Data flow languages', *Computer*, **15**.

A general introduction to the concepts of dataflow.

Aho, A. V., Sethi, R. and Ullman, J. D. 1986 *Compilers: Principles, Techniques and Tools*, Addison Wesley.

One of many books on the subject of compilers, but a personal favourite.

Almasi, George S. and Gottlieb, Allan 1989 *Highly Parallel Computing*, Benjamin Cumming.

Introduces foundations, software and architectures of parallel systems, with over 300 references!

America, Pierre, 'POOL' 1987 In *Object-Oriented Concurrent Programming*, A. Yonezawa (ed), MIT Press.

Details the object-oriented language POOL, developed under ESPRIT 415.

Anderson, A. 1965 'Program structures for parallel processing', *C.A.C.M.*, **8**, 786–788.

An early suggestion of the use of FORK and JOIN constructs.

Arvind, and Kathail, V. 1981 'A multiple processor dataflow machine that supports generalised procedures', *Computer Architecture News*, **9**, 291–302.

One of a number of papers by Arvind describing the dataflow work at MIT.

Baer, J. L. and Bovet, D. P. 1968 'Compilation of arithmetic expressions for parallel computation', *I.F.I.P. Congress Proceedings*, **1**, 340–6.

A technique for spreading arithmetic operations over a number of processors, based on a single left-to-right scan producing triples.

Ben-Ari, M. 1982 *Principles of Concurrent Programming*, Prentice Hall.

Lots of examples of ways of synchronizing the behaviour of processes. Includes details of fairness, liveness and starvation. Particularly good for mutual exclusion, semaphores and monitors.

Bernstein, A. 1966 'Analysis of Programs for Parallel Processing', *IEEE Transactions*, **EC15**, 757–763.

Studies the use of variables, introduces the classes W, X, Y and Z.

Bird, R. and Wadler, P. 1988 *Introduction to Functional Programming*, Prentice Hall.

A good introduction to the concepts of functional programming.

Birtwistle, Graham, M., Dahl, Ole-Johan, Myhrhaug, Bjorn, and Nygaard, Kristen 1973 *SIMULA BEGIN*, Petrocelli.

Introductory text for the simulation language Simula. Simula can be considered to be concurrent—if not truly parallel. Also worth considering as an early example of an object-oriented programming language.

Bolognesi, Tommaso and Brinksma, Ed. 1987 'Introduction to the ISO Specification Language LOTOS', *Computer Networks and ISDN Systems*, **14**, 25–59.

A good introduction to the essential parts of LOTOS; avoids some of the knottiness often associated with such specifications.

Boyle, James, Butler, Ralph, Disz, Terrence, Glickfield, Barnet, Lusk, Ewing, Overbeek, Ross, Patterson, James, and Stevens, Rick 1987 *Portable Programs for Parallel Processors*, Holt, Rinehart and Winston.

Lots of program examples and free software for trying them out.

Brown, P. (1988) *Software Portability*, Cambridge University Press.

A collection of papers discussing some of the issues of porting software, no mention of parallelism.

Carriero, Nicholas and Gelernter, David 1989 'Linda in Context', *C.A.C.M.*, **32**, 444–458.

Introduces the ideas of Linda and compares it (her) with (what they refer to as) the 'Big Three' parallel programming models: object oriented, logic and functional. N. B. Linda isn't a programming language—it is added to languages to make them parallel.

Chandy, K. Mani and Misra, Jayadev 1988 *Parallel Program Design—A Foundation*, Addison Wesley.

An excellent book (if somewhat difficult to read) that takes a formal approach, uses a small programming notation to express solutions to problems according to a number of parallel architectural models.

Clocksin, W. and Mellish, C. 1981 *Programming in Prolog*, Springer Verlag.

The book on Prolog.

Dennis, J. 1980 'Data flow supercomputers', *IEEE Computer*, **13**, 48–56.

Describes some of the original work on dataflow computers.

Dijkstra, E. W. 1975 'Guarded commands, nondeterminacy and formal derivation of programs', *C.A.C.M.*, **18**, 453–7.

Introduces non-determinacy into sequential programs via guarded commands.

Dijkstra, E. W. 1968 'Co-operating sequential processes'. In *Programming Languages*, F. Genuys (ed), Academic Press.

Introduces the P and V semaphores.

Evans, Christopher 1981 *The Making of the Micro—A History of the Computer*, Victor Gollancz Ltd.

The book of a TV series: all computer scientists should have read this book!

Evans, David J. 1982 *Parallel Processing Systems*, Cambridge University Press.

Lecture notes from an advanced course on parallel processing systems. Contains descriptions of the Loughborough Shared Memory Parallel Processor. Also contains notes on a number of other machines, algorithms and transformations.

Evans, D. J. and Smith, Shirley A. 1977 'On the construction of balanced binary trees for parallel processing', *Computer Journal*, **20**, 378–9.

One approach to dividing parts of (arithmetic) expressions over a number of processors.

Evans, D. J. and Williams, Shirley A. 1980 'Analysis and detection of parallel processable code', *Computer Journal*, **23**, 66–72.

Determines how variables are used in a process and uses this information to detect potential parallelism.

Flynn, Michael J. 1966 'Very high speed computing systems', *Proceedings of the I.E.E.E.*, **54**, 1901–9.

The original paper in which the terms SIMD and MIMD are defined.

Gill, S. 1958 'Parallel programming', *Computer Journal*, **1**, 2–10.

An early paper on the subject of parallel processing.

Gregory, S. 1987 *Parallel Logic Programming in PARLOG*, Addison Wesley.

An introduction to the parallel logic language PARLOG and ways in which it can be implemented.

Grosch, C. E. 1979 'Performance analysis of Poisson solvers on array computers'. In *Supercomputers* Hockney and Jesshope (eds).

Studies the performance of different algorithms on array processors linked in a variety of fashions.

Gurd, John, Kirkham, C. C., and Watson, I. 1985 'The Manchester prototype dataflow computer', *C.A.C.M.*, **28**, 34–52.

Describes the dataflow work at Manchester.

Handler, Wolfgang 1982 'Innovative computer architectures—how to increase parallelism but not complexity'. In *Parallel Processing Systems*, David J. Evans (ed), Cambridge University Press.

Describes the Erlangen classification system for existing and foreseeable computer systems.

Harland, David 1986 *Concurrency and Programming Languages*, Ellis Horwood.

Introduces an approach to the data abstraction that is close to many object-oriented styles. Studies how these can be used in sequential and concurrent contexts. Not light reading! The Rekursiv chipset is based on this.

Harland, David and Beloff, B. 1986 'Microcoding an object-oriented instruction set', *Computer Architecture News*, **14** (5) 3–12.

Introduces the Rekursiv chipset, designed to match an object-oriented language.

Hillis, W. Daniel 1985 *The Connection Machine*, The MIT Press.

An array processor architecture based on the semi-functional concepts of Common Lisp.

Hoare, C. A. R. 1978 'Communicating sequential processes', *C.A.C.M.*, **21**, 666–677.

Suggests input and output are basic primitives of parallel programming, along with guards and ∥.

Hoare, C. A. R. 1985 *Communicating Sequential Processes*, Prentice Hall.

Introduces the concept of communicating sequential processes. Describes operations and communications between them, along with ways of tracing actions and hiding events.

Hockney, Roger and Jesshope, Chris 1988 *Parallel Computers 2*, Adam Hilger.

The reference book for parallel computers. Contains details of most parallel computers, somewhat biased towards SIMD-type processing.

Hogger, Christopher J. 1984 *Introduction to Logic Programming*, Academic Press.

An introductory text to logic programming, with a final section on computing technology that addresses parallelism in logic.

Ibrahim, R. L., Ogden, J. A. and Williams, Shirley A. 1989 'Should Concurrency be Specified?'. In *Specification and Verification of Concurrent Systems*, BCS-FACS Workshop, vol. 1.

Discusses why and how software engineers should be expected to specify concurrency. Includes the maximum subsequence problem outlined in Chapter 1 as an example.

INMOS 1988 *occam 2 Reference Manual*, Prentice Hall.

Knuth, D. E. 1971 'An empirical study of Fortran programs', *Software Practice and Experience*, **1**, 105–33.

One of a number of studies on how programs are used. Supports the claims that arithmetic operations usually have few operands and programs spend most of their time in loops.

Kuck, David J. 1978 *The Structure of Computers and Computations*, vol. 1, John Wiley.

A number of sections on a variety of subjects, including processors, memories, networks and most interestingly (I think) a theoretical background to detection of parallelism.

Kuck, D. J., Muraoka,Y. and Chen, S. C. 1972 'On the number of operations simultaneously executable in Fortran-like programs and their resulting speed up', *I.E.E.E. Transactions on Computers*, **21**, 1293–310.

A technique for spreading arithmetic operations over a number of processors, including a suggestion of protection for delicate calculations.

Kung, H. T. 1982 'Notes on VLSI computation'. In *Parallel Processing Systems*, David J. Evans (ed), Cambridge University Press.

Describes the systolic array concept (details can also be found in Mead and Conway).

Mead, Carver and Conway, Lynn 1980 *Introduction to VLSI Systems*, Addison Wesley.

Excellent chapter on highly concurrent systems; with sections on processor organization, communications and algorithms.

Meyer, Bertrand 1988 *Object-oriented Software Construction*, Prentice Hall.

Describes the object-oriented approach to software engineering, including a section on concurrency.

Meyrowitz, N. 1986 'Proceedings of OOPSLA '86', *SIGPLAN*, **21**.

A collection of papers on object-oriented systems, languages and applications.

Perrott, R. H. 1987 *Parallel Programming*, Addison Wesley.

Describes a number of ways of achieving parallel programs, including Perrott's own language ACTUS.

Peyton-Jones, S. L. 1989 'Parallel implementations of functional programming languages', *Computer Journal*, **32**, 175–86.

A study of the suitability of functional programming languages for parallel processors.

Preparata, Franco P. 1987 *Parallel and Distributed Computing*, Advances in Computing Research, JAIP.

A collection of papers on aspects of parallel processing, including several on the PRAM concept.

Quinn, Michael J. 1987 *Designing Efficient Algorithms for Parallel Computers*, McGraw-Hill.

A comparison of the different approaches needed to exploit a variety of parallel architectures. Problems examined range from numeric to logic.

Refenes, Apostolos N. 1987 'Parallel computer architecture for symbolic and numeric processing', Ph.D Thesis, University of Reading.

Thesis on which the work for the ESPRIT project SPAN was conceived.

Roscoe, A. W. and Hoare, C. A. R. 1986 'The laws of occam programming', Programming Research Group, Oxford.

A basis for the automatic transformation of occam programs, based on the semantics defined here.

Shapiro, E. Y. 1986 'Concurrent Prolog', *Computer*, **19**, 44–58.

A variant on Prolog that allows representation of parallelism.

Stone, Harolds, 1987 *High Performance Computer Architecture*, Addison-Wesley.

Discusses in detail the architectures of many parallel machines.

Uhr, L. 1987 *Multi-Computer Architectures for Artificial Intelligence*, John Wiley.

Discusses the structure of a number of parallel processors and their use is efficiently solving problems in the field of Artificial Intelligence.

Ward, R. G. 1974 'A variable delay method for improving the recognition of parallel processable code in computer programs', *Computer Journal*, **17**, 157–64.

A technique for spreading several adjacent arithmetic expressions over a number of processors.

Whiddett, Dick 1987 *Concurrent Programming for Software Engineers*, Ellis Horwood.

Introduces programming styles for parallel processors. Concentrates on monitors, message and operation oriented systems.

Williams, Shirley A. 1979 'The portability of programs and languages for vector and array processors'. In *Supercomputers*, Infotech.

A proposal for a minimal machine to facilitate the transportation of programs between different array and/or vector processors.

Wirth, N. 1977 'Modula: A language for modular multiprogramming', *Software Practice and Experience*, **7**, 3–35.

Modula is the language on which Modula-2 is based: surprisingly Modula is the more parallel of the two.

Wirth, N. 1983. *Programming in Modula-2*, Springer Verlag.

The definitive text on Modula-2 (until the standard is complete). There are many other texts describing the language.

Index

DATE DUE

OCT 26 '95			
OCT 26 '94			
RET'D MAY 2 2 1995			
GAYLORD			PRINTED IN U.S.A.